How to Organize and Manage Your Art Room

Charles Comstock

illustrated by
Nicholas P. Soloway

J. WESTON
WALCH
PUBLISHER

PORTLAND, MAINE

User's Guide
to
Walch Reproducible Books

As part of our general effort to provide educational materials which are as practical and economical as possible, we have designated this publication a "reproducible book." The designation means that purchase of the book includes purchase of the right to limited reproduction of all pages on which this symbol appears:

Here is the basic Walch policy: We grant to individual purchasers of this book the right to make sufficient copies of reproducible pages for use by all students of a single teacher. This permission is limited to a single teacher, and does not apply to entire schools or school systems, so institutions purchasing the book should pass the permission on to a single teacher. Copying of the book or its parts for resale is prohibited.

Any questions regarding this policy or requests to purchase further reproduction rights should be addressed to:

Permissions Editor
J. Weston Walch, Publisher
321 Valley Street • P. O. Box 658
Portland, Maine 04104-0658

1   2   3   4   5   6   7   8   9   10

ISBN 0-8251-2651-7
Copyright © 1995
J. Weston Walch, Publisher
P. O. Box 658 • Portland, Maine 04104-0658

Printed in the United States of America

DEDICATION

I would like to dedicate this book
to my wife and children,
who put up with me
during its writing.

Contents

Foreword

For the purpose of this book, the art classroom should be a space that contains the following:

- heating, cooling, and lighting systems

- storage space for art supplies

- work areas for students

- a cleanup area with a water supply

- a blackboard of some type

- a desk for the teacher

- counter and shelf space

Hopefully, all of the above items will be in the room when you are assigned to it. But be prepared for the worst.

When my principal first showed me the art classroom, I was pleased to see plenty of cabinet space, a large sink, a large blackboard, several easels, a vertical file storage unit, and what appeared to be a lot of art supplies. But was I ever surprised that summer day I went to school to do some work in my room! The drain was clogged. The paint bottle lids had not been tightly closed, so the paint had dried and couldn't be saved. There were odd amounts of various types of paper. The blackboard had all sorts of strange sticky things on it. The cabinets were coming loose from the wall. There was a large mass of yarn that was heavier than it looked. Later, I found the enameling kiln inside this ball of yarn.

With a lot of elbow grease, I was able to correct the problem areas in about two weeks. That was the easy work.

I soon came to realize that students took advantage of any opportunity to make off with anything not nailed down, or not checked in some way before the end of each class. Materials placed on the tables for students to use became easy prey or something for someone else to clean up. I was amazed at how fast a student can say, "I cleaned mine" or "I didn't use it."

I hope that you do have a room that is adequate for the teaching of art and the organization and storage of supplies. The ideas in this book should help you turn a less than ideal space into a more workable, practical one.

To the Teacher

Teachers today can find books in just about any area of interest. If you're looking for new lessons for your subject area—no problem! There are many sources, from your local library to a mail-order publisher.

But start to look for a book on classroom organization and you'll find a different situation. There are few books readily available. For some reason, publishers assume that a future teacher will know how to go about organizing his or her classroom. The truth is, most of a teacher's training will deal with special behavioral problems, child psychology, the curriculum, and so on. Teachers usually are not taught classroom organization in college, and when they enter their classrooms for the first time, they have to go it alone.

There are several ways to learn how to organize a classroom and its procedures. Among them are:

- advice from experienced teachers
- trial and error
- observation of other teachers

My guess is that new teachers use some combination of these methods. What one art teacher does in his or her room may not always work for another, for whatever reason. Art may be one of the most troublesome subjects around which to organize a classroom. Space, budget, grade levels, and media all come into play.

It is my intent to help art teachers become better organized within their classrooms. The material in this book is the product of my 22 years of experience teaching high school art. I'm still using everything in this book in my art classroom today.

If you are just starting out as an art teacher, I hope that this book will help make it possible for you to enjoy teaching art.

—*Charles W. Comstock, Jr.*

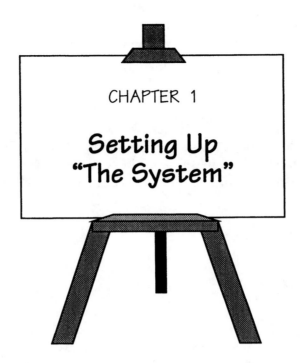

CHAPTER 1

Setting Up "The System"

However you choose to organize your art classroom, the following objectives are basic:

1. maintaining the art equipment, supplies, and tools

2. keeping breakage to a minimum

3. achieving maximum on-task time

4. reducing theft of supplies

5. promoting classroom safety

6. reducing the confusion during a lesson

I arrived at my organizational system by trial and error. Some attempts at organization were total failures. Others worked better than I anticipated. Sometimes my solutions created more problems to be solved. Nevertheless, I eventually reached a method that does work for me. I devised an organizational system that I call, imaginatively, "The System."

Any art teacher can modify this system to his or her individual situation. The first thing you need is either a willingness to do construction work or a good relationship with your school's shop teacher.

Storage Trays

The first order of business is to purchase plastic shoe-box-size containers. You can usually get these at a department store for about a dollar. A similar item is what is called a parts bin box. You can get parts bin boxes through office supply companies for under a dollar each. They are not as durable as plastic shoe boxes, but they work.

Here is a drawing of these two items:

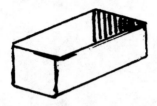

Plastic shoe box

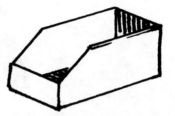

Cardboard parts tray

You must have enough of these trays for your largest class. It would be ideal to have one for every student you teach.

Supply Counter

The next item in The System is the supply counter. The counter will store the supply trays between classes. This is where your relationship with the shop teacher is important. If you don't have a shop teacher at your school, then you must build the counter.

When I started designing and building my first counter (I now have two), I had all kinds of student help, since I was building it within my classroom. Perhaps you can enlist some student labor. If you do, reward your helpers in some way; then they will be readily available when you attempt other building projects.

Following is a drawing of the supply counter, with its cubbyholes for the trays. Construction plans for the supply counter are given in Chapter 6, pages 95–101.

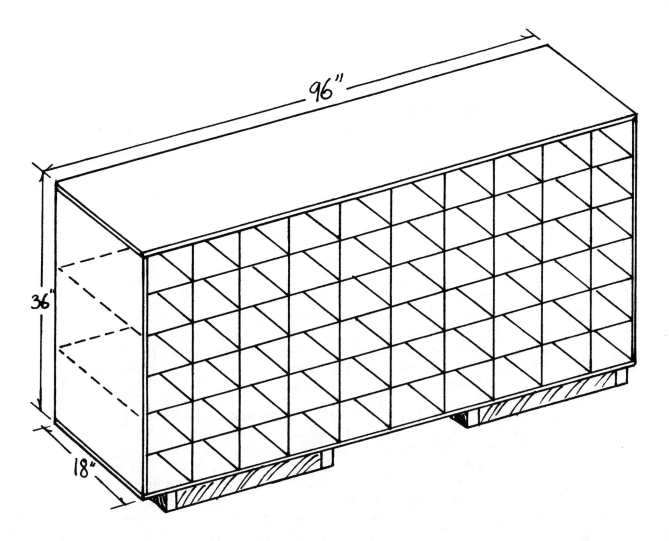

Supply counter

• • • • • •

By now, you may be wondering how some boxes and a counter can be called a system. Basically, each tray contains the art tools for any particular lesson, and the trays are all stored in the counter. I know you're thinking that you've seen this in many art supply catalogs. But what is available is usually too big and the cost is too high for those of us on limited art budgets. Besides, those units don't come with all the practical tips you'll find in this book.

Let's go to work setting up the system. First, you must find a place to put the supply counter. You could place it against a wall, or it could be in the middle of the room. For many years I arranged my supply counter and desk so that they enclosed a small area within the room. During that time I used a regular teacher desk. Now, I use a desk I designed that encloses its own space within the room.

How to Use "The System"

Here is how you can use The System in the classroom. First, determine how many students you have within each class you teach during one school day. Let's say, for example, that you have 76 Art I students, 23 Art II students, and 19 Art III students. For the Art I classes, say you have 22 students during the first period, 25 students in second period, and 29 students in third period. Therefore, you'll need 29 Art I trays (the maximum number of Art I students you teach at one time), 23 Art II trays, and 19 Art III trays. That's a total of 71 trays.

Now, we'll look at a "trial run" using The System.

1. In first period Art I, you have 22 students. Assign each student a tray, 1 through 22, that he or she will use all year. Tell students that they are responsible for all the tools in their tray. If something is missing or was left dirty by the previous class (in this case, sixth period from the previous day), students must tell you at the beginning of the class. Students may not change or share trays unless you authorize it. Take the roll and give instructions for the period, then have students start work.

2. Near the end of the period, ask the class to clean up. Each student must now clean his or her tools and put them back in the tray and then place the tray on the supply counter. An aide then checks the contents before placing the tray in its cubby. If something is missing or not clean, the aide should tell the student. All trays must be put away before you allow the class to leave.

3. Second period begins, and each class member takes a seat. You take the roll and give instructions. Again, each student gets an assigned tray. Since you have 25 students in this class, you will assign three additional trays. Trays 1 through 22 will be shared with the first-period class. Cleanup rules are the same as before.

4. Third period requires 29 trays—the 25 you have used so far, plus four additional trays. Now all trays for Art I are assigned.

5. The bell rings and third period ends. All trays have been put away. The 23 Art II students are entering the room and taking their seats. You will assign each of these students a tray lettered A through W. They will be the only students using these trays.

6. It is now your final class of the day, Art III. At this point you have assigned 52 trays. The supply counter has 60 trays, and you need 19 for Art III. Unless you have built an additional or bigger supply counter (you may have to start small for budget reasons), you can either assign shared trays, or you can wait a while before assigning

trays. The beginning of the school year always comes with schedule changes. Your class size may change. If it becomes smaller, your problem may be solved. When you do assign trays, you can double-letter them (AA, BB, etc.) to distinguish them from the Art I and Art II trays.

The scenario will be the same every day of the school year, unless you have a lesson that does not require a tray. A master list of tray assignments will help keep you on track.

What really makes the above plan work for me is the teacher aides. I use student teacher-aides to hand out and check in supply trays. I have two aides assigned to each period, so that if one is absent, I still have one to help me out. At one time, a student in our school could earn half a credit as an aide. Now I check with the study hall teacher and see if any students would like to be an aide for me.

If you can't get students from outside your class to help you, you could have students from your class serve as aides for one week each. Make out a schedule. I always assign two students per week. I give the aides an extra daily grade, or some other type of grade, each week.

Aides are helpful, but they sometimes forget to check for missing or dirty tools. So I check trays one day each week. It is never the same day. And one week I may be checking for cleanliness, the next week that all assigned tools are in the tray. I give a grade of 100 for that day to each student whose tray passes muster. If anyone is absent, I check the tray when he or she comes back. This checkup doesn't completely solve the problem of dirty or missing items, but it does help.

If you can get or build two supply counters, you can assign students their own supply trays. Many teachers don't have room in their budgets or their classrooms for more than one counter or for the extra tools and supplies that more trays require, but if you can do it, so much the better.

For many years I worked with only one supply counter. But one year I decided that I had had enough of students complaining about dirty or missing tools. I had some money left in my art budget, so I decided to construct another supply counter and buy additional plastic trays.

Constructing the supply counter was difficult, but I always had plenty of helpers. I wasn't ready for the relatively high cost of the plastic shoe boxes. The cardboard parts trays proved to be a good solution. Since these trays cost under a dollar, if one is damaged and can't be used the next year, you haven't lost that much.

Storage of Artwork

Once students have started creating some two-dimensional work, you are faced with finding a safe place to keep it from one day to the next. Most art catalogues offer different types of racks for storing and drying artwork, but often they are too large or too expensive for your needs.

For many years I used a wooden frame with chicken wire stretched over it to create drying racks. The problem was, students in other classes would see work lying on the rack and pick it up to look at it or to show others. Then they would forget where they found the piece and put it back in the wrong place. If the artist was not popular with the student holding the piece, the artwork might simply disappear. My blood pressure would reach 200 over 200 when this happened. Even today I give a good chewing out to any student who is handling another's work without permission.

One day while I was looking through an art magazine, I saw an article on how to store large sheets of paper in a slotted unit. I realized that I could build a similar unit to hold student artwork.

SLOTTED STORAGE UNIT

The slotted storage unit (see following illustration) has worked out well.

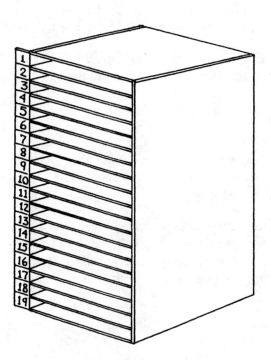

Slotted storage area

Student work is protected from the prying eyes of others. Occasionally, someone will remove a piece of artwork, but this happens much less often than it did with the chicken wire frames.

Construction plans for this storage unit are in Chapter 6, page 102. The units I built are big enough for the largest paper my students work on during the year. You would probably want to build yours the same way. You might also want to build enough units so that each student can have his or her own slot.

Keep in mind that you also need an area, preferably a counter, where the units can sit. I have a wide counter that stretches across the back of my classroom for the seven units my students use.

Classroom Layout

My classroom layout is shown on the following page. Each classroom is different, of course, so you may have to place the storage units in several different areas around your room. If so, you can assign students storage units that are near their regular work areas. This can actually help prevent bottlenecks when students are picking up or storing artwork.

I caution you about placing the slotted storage units on top of the supply counter. I tried this one year and it did not work as I had planned. However, it may work for you.

Here is how you would assign slots for students to put their work in when you are using only one supply counter. Since you have more storage slots than trays, you will need to do one of several things. Each student will have been assigned a *numbered* tray, as explained earlier. However, when you assign *slots*, you assign each student a slot that has a number with a *letter*. As an example, the student in first period who has been assigned to tray 10 will also use slot 10A. The A will be on *all slots* for first-period students only. So when that student is ready to get his supply tray, he asks for tray 10 for his tools and slot 10A for his art work.

The same thing would be done for second period, except that the letter would be a B instead of an A. The B is used because it is the second letter of the alphabet. Slot numbers would be 1B, 2B, 3B, 4B, etc.

You will have to label the Art II trays and slots differently than those for Art I. These could simply have a letter for the tray and slot such as A, B, C, . . . However, if you have more than one Art II class, you would have to use a different system, such as higher numbers with a letter for each of these two periods: 30D, 31D, etc. . . . The D would stand for the fourth-period Art II class, since D is the fourth letter of the alphabet. The other Art II class would be assigned trays and slots the same way, but with a different letter, such as F for sixth-period Art II.

Art Room Layout

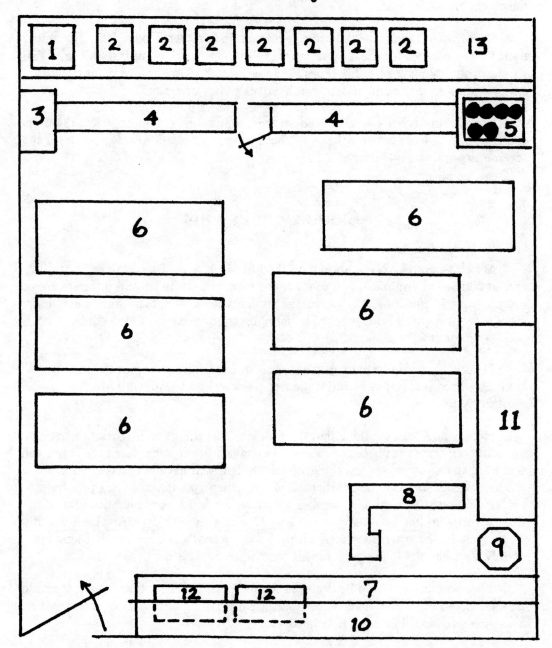

1. spray box
2. slotted storage units
3. file cabinet
4. supply counters
5. paint supply area
6. worktables
7. counter with cabinets
8. my desk
9. kiln
10. cabinets
11. counter with lower cabinets
12. sinks
13. counter

Double letters for the Art III students would probably be all you would need to use, unless of course you have more than one Art III class.

The various techniques described above are methods I've used over the years when assigning trays and slots. You might find another way to use them. If it works for you, that's great!

CHAPTER 2

Methods and Hints for Various Media

Working with Tempera

In most studio art courses, students paint throughout the year. Once you have determined how often your students will be painting, you can structure your curriculum so that painting lessons are grouped together. This will save you the bother of changing the tools in each student's tray every few weeks. I do most lessons that require brushes, a paint tray, and a water container in the first semester. I do crafts and sculpture lessons, which may not require paint, in the second semester.

To set up the supply trays for painting, first determine exactly which tools you want students to have available. For example:

- a large (size 7) brush

- a small (size 3) brush

- a water container (an 8- to 10-ounce plastic cup)

- a round, plastic, 10-well paint tray

Then do the following:

1. Mark each size brush with colored tape for easy identification. That is, use one color tape for the large brushes and another color for the smaller brushes.

2. Mark each paint tray with the same letter or number as the supply tray it is stored in.

3. Mark each plastic water cup with the number or letter of the supply tray.

4. Assemble the trays.

Now you're ready to start a painting lesson—almost. I'd like to mention a few problems you might encounter when you turn students loose with paint.

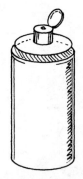

Paint container collar

The first problem concerns the container you use to dispense tempera. I have tried various types over the last 22 years, from squeeze bottles to gallon containers with pumps.

With the squeeze bottle, paint often drips from the opening each time a student uses it. The paint starts running down the sides of the bottle, creating a mess. I've come up with a partial solution. The diagram on the left shows a cardboard collar with a center hole cut just large enough to fit over the top of the bottle when the cover is off. This keeps paint from running down the sides of the bottle. But you do have to change the collar every couple of weeks.

With a gallon-size pump container, watch out for clogs of dried paint in the spout. When my students were having trouble one day, I attempted to clear the clog and then pump some paint. The paint came out suddenly onto the paint tray— and onto my shirt. The same thing happened to some students several days later. I realized I'd better come up with a solution fast.

First, I saw that something had to be placed over the spout to keep the paint in it from drying out overnight. Tape was an easy solution to that. Next, I constructed an enclosure for the paint containers (see illustration, right). The front is lower than the sides and back, which allows the students to place their paint trays right underneath the spouts. I also stapled a strip of poster board to the top edge of the front as a splash guard. This enclosure has greatly reduced paint splattering in my classroom.

Gallon paint container enclosure

REDUCING PAPER TOWEL USE

For years, paper towels put quite a dent in my art budget, and I sometimes ran out of them before the end of the school year. Then I realized that newspaper works just as well for drying paint brushes. I now cut old papers into three- or four-inch strips and place them next to the paint dispenser.

I also purchased several cheap bath towels and cut them in half. I place these near the sink area and instruct students to use them for drying their cleaned paint trays, water containers, and other tools. They now use paper towels only to dry their hands.

Working with Printing Tools and Materials

BLOCK PRINTING

Most art teachers want their students to explore the printing process. Perhaps the most common lesson is in block printing, with either a wood or a linoleum block. These are both easy to use.

During the education of an art teacher, the process of block printing is usually covered. But this doesn't really prepare you for your first experience in teaching block printing. I know I sure wasn't ready. There's something about being in a classroom with 25 or more individuals who are all holding something that can cause bodily harm that gives you pause. Even if you show them how to carve the block safely, you may still see some minor injuries.

Year after year I tried to figure out how I could prevent injuries. Then I found the answer—block holders. You can make these with any type of wood. The diagrams below show left- and right-handed block holders. Construction plans are in Chapter 6, page 109.

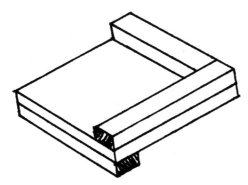

Left-handed block holder

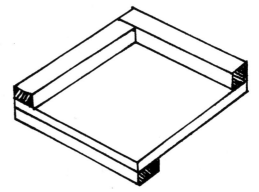

Right-handed block holder

The block holder allows the student to place the hand not carving out of harm's way.

ORGANIZING THE TOOLS

If students are sharing supply trays, put the following items into each tray:

- a size 1 linoleum carving tool

- a size 3 linoleum carving tool

- a size 5 linoleum carving tool

- a hard rubber brayer (4-inch or 6-inch)

Mark each of the carving tools with a different color of tape. Then your student aides can quickly determine if any tools are missing. Place the other items students need—printing ink, paper, and metal inking plates—behind the supply counter and distribute as needed.

Even if you have a supply tray for every student, it may be too costly to have carving tools for each one. Here is another way to organize the distribution, without using trays. First, determine how many students you think will be carving at any one time. In my class, it's about 12. So I set out 12 carving tools in each size. Then I take a permanent marker and number the tools. I number size 1 tools 1 through 12. I number size 3 tools 30 through 41, and I number size 5 tools 50 through 61. With this system, I can tell carving tool size with a glance at the number.

Use a signout sheet (Chapter 3, page 41) to keep track of the tools students are using. I don't allow my student aides to hand out carving tools. It's too easy for a tool to disappear. At cleanup time, I sit at my desk and scratch out the students' names as they return their carving tools to me personally. Once I have all the tools, I put them out of reach until the next class.

TWO-COLOR BLOCK PRINTS

I know a lot of art teachers would like to present a two-color block printing lesson, but you can't always pick up the method at college. The process is not very different from one-color block printing, except that the two blocks must be perfectly aligned so that the colors fit together to form one print.

Over the years I experimented with different ways to align the blocks, but all failed in one way or another. Then I started using what I call a printing block, which looks like a block holder with an extra, stepped-back strip. Construction plans are in Chapter 6, page 111.

Here are the steps I follow to make a two-color block print.

1. Create a design that uses two different colors. Draw the whole design on a wood or linoleum carving block.

2. Decide which color in the design will be on the first block. Then carve off all other parts.

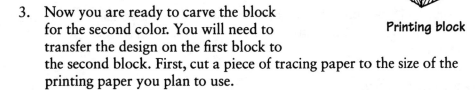

Printing block

3. Now you are ready to carve the block for the second color. You will need to transfer the design on the first block to the second block. First, cut a piece of tracing paper to the size of the printing paper you plan to use.

4. With ink, a roller, and an inking plate, ink the first block and place it face up into the lower corner of the printing block.

5. Place the tracing paper into the upper corner formed by the wooden strips on the printing block. With one finger, gently rub the back of the tracing paper so that the first block prints onto it.

6. Remove the first block and set it aside.

7. Place the second block into the same position you used for the first block. Carefully lay the tracing paper print on the second block. Again, align it against the wooden strip with the inked side down.

8. Gently rub the tracing paper to transfer the design to the second block. Then remove the tracing paper and discard it.

9. Now you can see where the design for the first block is in relation to the second block. Draw the remaining parts of the design on the second block. Then carve away the parts that are not needed for the second color.

10. Now you have two blocks ready for printing. You can print several copies of the first block with your first color. Allow the ink on those sheets to dry. Then ink the second block with the second color and print the same pieces of paper, making sure to line up the paper and second block correctly.

OTHER TYPES OF PRINTING

If you want your class to do a screen print, you have to consider the type of ink and blockout solution you will use. You must have adequate ventilation for printing with oil-based ink. You might set aside one or two days of the week to print the screens. That would reduce the amount of time your students are exposed to the ink fumes.

Oil-based blockout solution also gives off fumes. I recommend a water-based blockout, since students will be using it on a daily basis. You could still use an oil-based ink.

You must also determine what you are going to do at cleanup time. If you want students to clean their own screens, use nonflammable, nonfuming cleanup solution.

Lithography printing has the same cleanup requirements as screen printing. Consider ventilation and cleanup time when planning both screen printing and lithography lessons.

STRETCHING SCREENS

For several years, at the end of the screen printing lessons, I would be faced with stretching new screens onto the wooden frames for the next school year. I sometimes had student help, but I ended up doing most of the work myself.

Then I hit upon the solution, which had been staring me in the face all the time. I require each art student to stretch a new screen after his or her printing is concluded. I give each student a grade for this task. To get a score of 100, the student must stretch the screen tight enough for a coin to bounce off it.

You would be amazed at how much students get into this. When someone has finished stretching a screen, they can't wait to try bouncing a coin off it.

Now I don't have to take time out from my teaching to accomplish or supervise screen stretching. And this task gives students a better understanding of the screen printing process.

Handing Out Paper

As I found out during my first few years as a teacher, a ream of paper can do a disappearing act that would top the best magician.

When I first started, I would set paper on one corner of my desk for students to take. As my class sizes became larger, I became aware of how much paper we were using.

As part of each lesson, I asked students to use both sides of each sheet. I also moved the paper from my desk to behind the supply counter. Yet it seemed like students were still using too much paper. I'm not talking about cheap manila or newsprint. Eighty-pound all-media, parchment, and watercolor paper are a major expense for most art classes. We have to use them carefully.

I had always asked students to make small preliminary drawings. Then they would come to my desk and get a sheet of good paper for their final product. Students often bypassed the first step, however, so I had to start requiring that they get my initials on their preliminary drawing before an aide would issue a sheet of paper from behind the supply counter. I did this so that I could move around the classroom while students were working.

That worked fine. But now I just ask students to show me their preliminary drawing, and then I give them a sheet of paper from a shelf in my custom-built teacher desk. Sometimes I let students get the paper themselves, but they must ask permission first.

My desk suits my personal needs as a teacher. It is like the supply counter, except that it has several drawers, shelves, and various small compartments. The shelves allow me to store various sizes of paper and other supplies. The three sections of my desk are shown below.

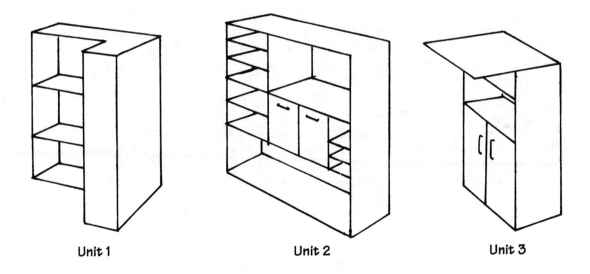

Unit 1　　　　　　　　Unit 2　　　　　　　　Unit 3

The corner unit (1) has three shelves. The second unit has two drawers in the center, a large open shelf on the bottom, and other shelves of different sizes. The third unit has a bottom cabinet that can be locked, and two large shelves. It also has a work area on top.

Working with Pen and Ink

Pen and ink is a basic art lesson. But of course, it comes with a few potential problems. Adolescents are sometimes a bit clumsy, and ink bottles are small. When these two conditions meet, accidents happen.

Ink bottle caps can also be tricky. Regardless of the bargain price, don't buy the kind of bottle that has a rubber top that pushes into the bottle, much like a cork in a wine bottle. Students often don't push the cap in completely. The ink cakes around the opening, causing the cap to come off easily. Students carry the bottles by their caps, and you know what happens next. Bottles with screw-on caps are much better.

I also have a way to avoid tipping accidents. Cut out three-inch squares of cardboard (from the backs of used notebooks or pads) and glue one to the bottom of each ink bottle. This gives it a more stable base.

KEEPING TRACK OF MEDIA

Set out ink bottles in a place where you can keep an eye on them. Tape a large piece of white paper on this counter. Rule it into squares about the size of the cardboard ink bases, and then number each square. Then you can tell at a glance if all of the ink bottles have been returned. If you were putting out 12 bottles of ink, you would number the squares 1 through 12.

For different colors of ink, you can do something similar. If you were setting out three bottles of ink for each color, you could write the name of the color on the sheet of white paper in front of the first bottle in each row of color. Divide each row into three squares and number each row from 1 to 3. Then you could quickly see if you have all three bottles of each color at the end of the class.

Students quickly see that you're using the honor system. If you're missing a bottle, all you need to do is say so. Usually, someone has just forgotten to return it.

Now to pens. I make a small tag for each pen; you can use things like manila-folder labels, fluorescent labels, or masking tape. Wrap the sticker around the top of the pen, leaving enough out to make a small "flag" about an inch long. What you write on the flag may depend on the lesson you're working on.

For a calligraphy lesson:

1. Select the pens you will set out for student use. Examples: A-1, A-3, A-5, B-0, B-3, B-5, etc.

2. Determine approximately how many pens of any one size may be in use at any given time. Example: five A-1s, five A-3s, five A-5s, etc.

3. Find containers for each pen size you are setting out. They will be placed near the bottles of ink. Tape a small label with the designated pen size (A-1, A-3, etc.) in front of each container. Tape the containers down to keep them from tipping over.

4. Write the pen size (A-1, A-3) on each pen's flag.

5. Put out a sign-out sheet (see Chapter 3, page 41) for the pens and ink bottles. Students will scratch out their names when they return the materials.

6. For pen cleaning, put a container filled with pen cleaner at the sink. Instruct students to clean their pens, rinse out the cleaner with plain water, and dry the clean pen nib on a rag.

This drill would be the same for every day you teach calligraphy.

For a pen and ink drawing lesson the procedure would be the same, except the flags on the crow quill pens would have numbers instead of pen sizes. If you were setting out 12 quill pens, you would number them 1 through 12. Then the students would write the number of the pen they were using on the sign-out sheet for the period.

This procedure may seem time-consuming on first reading. But it really isn't. Besides, keeping track of your expensive art supplies is worth it. If you see lots of people using ink and pens, but only a few are signed out, just mention that you'll be deducting points from students' daily grades. It works every time.

END-OF-YEAR CLEANUP

At the end of the school year, you have to do four things with the ink bottles:

1. Pour out the remaining ink. If you left it in for next year, it would cake around the cap and possibly dry up anyway.

2. Place the bottles in a bucket of water for several hours or overnight. This softens the glue so that you can remove it and the cardboard squares.

3. Clean the ink bottles and let them dry.

4. Cut new cardboard squares and glue them onto the bottles. Now you're ready for next year!

Working with Sprays

Spray fixatives (like those used for charcoal, pastel, and pencil drawings), spray paints, and certain types of gloss sprays all create fumes that can be extremely harmful if inhaled long enough and often enough. As an art teacher, you must figure out how to use these sprays so that your students don't leave class with something other than a creative high. Students and teachers with respiratory problems or allergies must also be protected.

Most sprays have label instructions on how to use them and what precautions to take. Most recommend "adequate" ventilation. But many modern school buildings don't have a lot of windows. Even if your room does have numerous windows, the smell may still linger for several periods.

At one point, I was taking artwork into the hallway to spray fixative or ceramic gloss. Teachers nearby had to close their doors to avoid the smell. Then I started going outside the building, which was time consuming and inconvenient. Sometimes I would let a student go outside to use the spray. But after some students redecorated the outside of the ROTC trailer, I had to stop letting students go outside. (Funny, not one of my students who were outside at the time saw who added the artistic improvements to the ROTC trailer.)

I started looking through art supply catalogs for a spray enclosure that I could afford, in vain. I worked up a design that I thought would be functional and cost less. With the help of the shop teacher, I purchased the materials for less than forty dollars. On the next page is the design for my simple spray box. The construction plans are in Chapter 6, on pages 112–114.

CAUTION:

Always check with your school administration for any regulations regarding hazardous substances.

My spray box uses a bathroom vent fan to exhaust the fumes to the exterior of the building. The exhaust pipe is four-inch stovepipe. The unit is wired so that it can be plugged into a nearby electrical outlet.

To operate, open the window and turn the exhaust pipe outward (assuming you didn't make a permanent opening in the wall, which is also an option). Turn on the fan and then place the object to be sprayed inside, and start spraying. A cake-decorating turntable is a good addition when the object you're spraying must be turned to be thoroughly covered. This costs less than the turntables sold in art catalogs.

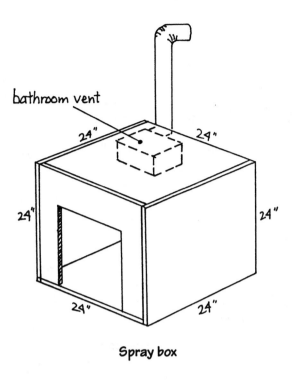

Spray box

Mat Cutting

Matting artwork improves the look of the work in many ways. It isolates the work from its surroundings; it makes the work look more professional; and it adds to the overall aesthetic appeal.

Art teachers usually don't mat most student work unless it is being submitted for a contest. The expense of mat board is one reason. Time is another. But I believe that work should be matted regardless of the reason it was created. To cut down on the cost, I use the following types of paper:

- poster board that is white on one side

- tagboard

- old poster board (you could always paint it)

To get students into doing their own matting, you could:

- use purchased, precut mats

- draw out the measurements on the blackboard, and have students measure and cut their own mats

- make a mat pattern with heavy cardboard, and have students trace the pattern on their mats and then cut out the mats

The last two options require you to give a lesson in mat cutting. Let's say you have decided to teach mat cutting to your advanced students. Here is how you can organize it so that you can keep track of the tools.

1. Establish an area near your desk for all mat cutting. That way, you can easily check progress and hand out tools.

2. Place the mat board nearby, so that aides can hand it out or students can pick it up themselves.

3. Have students sign out the mat knife, and then hand it to them. Cross off their names when they hand it back in. I always instruct my students to give the knife back to me and not to another student. This is extra work for me, but I do it for the safety of the other students and myself.

4. Students can use scissors on poster board and tagboard. I hammered several pairs of nails into the side of my supply cabinet. I hung a pair of scissors over each pair of nails and traced the shape of the scissors with a marker. The aides hand out scissors as needed, and we can tell at a glance how many pairs are out. If you don't use aides, you can hang the scissors in the same fashion somewhere behind your desk and hand them out yourself.

You may think this is going too far with organizing tools, but if a pair of scissors comes up missing and you ask for its whereabouts, the answer is usually, "Not me! I didn't take them."

Second- and third-year students are generally more responsible than kids who are taking your class for the first time. With the systems described here, sometimes all it takes is a quick look to be sure all tools are put away.

Working with Ceramics

If there is any area of art teaching that requires good organizational skills, it's ceramics. I hope you'll find lots of ideas in this chapter. But first, let's talk about kilns. A kiln is a major purchase for any art department. If you don't have enough money in your budget, maybe you can convince your principal to help with the cost.

ACQUIRING A KILN

You will have to present your principal with well-thought-out information. Consider the following:

1. You must determine where in your art room or school you can place the kiln. It should be an area that is at some distance from your students' everyday work area.

2. You must determine the electrical requirements for the kiln you plan to purchase. If your room or area already has an adequate electrical outlet, you'll save on the cost of an electrician.

3. You must be able to talk about the dependability and serviceability of the kiln you want to buy. With luck, it will never need any repairs. If it does, you may be the one doing them.

4. Be prepared to talk about how you will use the kiln. Stress that it will allow you to expand the curriculum within the courses that you already teach. You could also offer to expand overall course offerings by teaching ceramic courses one or two periods a day. This will add to the success and prestige of your art program, making the school look good in the process.

If you don't succeed in convincing your principal to help you buy a kiln, you could always have your students' clay projects fired at a local ceramic shop or pottery works. These shops will usually do the firing at a reduced price for schools.

For the purpose of this book, I will outline organizational material assuming that you have the use of a kiln in one way or another.

ORGANIZING CERAMIC LESSONS

If art course offerings at your school include levels such as Art I, Art II, and Art III, consider dividing ceramic lessons by technique.

I teach ceramic casting to my Art I students. They use tempera or underglazes to decorate their objects. Art II students do ceramic casting, but they also explore modeling by creating a clay face. I introduce Art III students to slab, coil, and pinch pots, as well as the pottery wheel. They also learn about different types of glazes.

This section on ceramics will be divided into these three areas:

*   ceramic casting

*   clay modeling

*   hand techniques such as slab, coil, pinch, and the wheel

CERAMIC CASTING

Setting Up the Classroom

1. In advance of the class (probably beginning several weeks beforehand, to allow yourself plenty of time), prepare a finished example of each mold you will be using. You don't have to decorate the molds. The purpose is just to show students what the clay figures look like. Otherwise, you'll spend too much class time describing them. Give each object a name for easy reference.

2. Since you may have only one ceramic mold for each object your students will make, you must determine which students will cast from which molds on each day of the lesson. (Remember that a ceramic mold should only be used once every 24 hours.) I've designed a form that all students complete. On this form, students list at least four different molds that they would like to cast. Then I select who will be casting the next day for each period. This allows me to rotate the most popular molds in each class.

3. Choose an area of your classroom adequate for setting out molds and having several students cast at one time.

4. Set out at least six half-gallon containers of slip. Plastic pitchers work perfectly and are inexpensive.

5. You'll also need a small bucket of water in which to put scrap pieces of clay or broken projects so they can be recycled. The scraps will soften in water, and you can beat them with a portable mixer so they can be used again. This saves quite a bit of money.

6. Also on the casting table, place a container of paper slips on which students can write their names to put with their clay objects.

7. Another container can hold five or six wooden ceramic tools, which are used to remove excess slip that gets on the clay mold during the casting process.

Now you're ready to start casting. I generally choose people who have finished with the previous project to begin this one.

Check the inside of each mold for any potential problems. Then set it with the form that each student has filled out. You may want to ask the students if they are happy with the molds that have been set out for them. If some of them have changed their minds (especially if they didn't get their first choice), some swapping may take place.

The process of casting can be broken into various steps, depending on how detailed you want to get. Here's a basic procedure.

The Casting Process

1. Check the mold for the number of parts to be filled with slip.

2. Remove the lid from a container of slip and stir to restore an even consistency (the clay tends to settle).

3. Put the lid back on.

4. Pour the slip slowly into the ceramic mold.

5. Leave the slip in the mold for a set amount of time. (Time varies depending on the mold. You must determine what the times are and post them where students can see them.)

6. Add slip as it goes down while in the mold.

7. After the required time period, slowly pour the slip back into the container. Allow the slip to completely drain from the mold by setting it over the container for 4-5 minutes.

8. After the mold stops dripping, place it on the table, and with the wooden tool, remove any slip that has gotten on the outside of the mold.

9. Have each student write his or her name on a piece of paper and place it under the rubber band on the mold, then puts the mold in a designated safe place. The student then cleans his or her work area.

Later, you will remove the clay objects from the molds and put the students' name tags under their objects. During the next class meeting, students will use ceramic cleanup tools and sponges to remove mold seams and any rough areas. Then they will decorate the objects with whatever glazes or paints you provide.

If you plan to use ceramic glazes, you will need a glaze chart so students can make their selections. You can also use ceramic stains, tempera, or acrylic paint.

If your art program includes different levels, such as I, II, and III, I recommend that you introduce the many and varied ceramic glazes in stages. In an introductory course, the students could learn the basic concepts of glazing. Then they could move on to advanced and special glazing techniques in subsequent courses.

Casting and decorating clay objects is safe for all classes exploring this area of art. I encourage my students to go to local ceramics shops and see what else they can find.

CLAY MODELING

You can use many different clay forms and figures to teach modeling technique. Some examples:

- the human figure

- a realistic animal

- an imaginary animal or figure

- a lifelike human face

- a mask

At one time or another I have used all of these as a lesson in my Art II program. Whichever you use, you will need all of the items listed below:

- Several pieces of canvas for the students to work on every day

- Various wooden or plastic ceramic tools

- At least 5 pounds of earthenware clay per student. (High-firing clay may be too costly.)

- Various materials to form armatures for any student who might need them. These could include old newspaper, cardboard, paper towels, wire, etc.

- Wooden rolling pins to roll out the slabs of clay. You need at least one per table. It is best to remove the handles to begin with, because they'll come loose eventually and could cause injury.

- Sheets of plastic. You could cut trash bags or plastic shopping bags into various sizes.

How will you distribute the ceramic tools? If students share supply trays, place a set of tools in each tray, marking tools with different colors of tape for easy identification.

If students have their own supply trays, it may be too expensive to supply tools for each one. You can set up enough ceramic tool sets for at least half the students in your largest class. Put each set into a numbered container of some type. You can place these containers either behind the supply counter to be handed out by an aide, or near your desk. Provide a sign-out sheet.

One more thing to consider is the minimum and maximum size of the objects your students will create. You'll usually have someone who wants to make something really tiny, and someone else who wants to make something monumental. Remember that you must be able to fit these clay forms into a kiln.

Modeling is a project that most students enjoy. And it's interesting for you, too. You can quickly see who is able to visualize a three-dimensional form and then create it.

HAND TECHNIQUES

For the slab method, coil method, and pinch method, you will need:

- Several pairs of guide sticks to use when rolling out clay—I use $\frac{3}{8}$-inch plywood strips, about 2 inches by 16 inches in size.

- A source of slip that students can use to join two pieces of clay

- Several old brushes with which they can apply the slip

All tools would be behind the supply counter, to be handed out as needed. Give each student the clay that he or she will need. I have students show me a picture from a book or a drawing of what they would like to do.

If you have a pottery wheel, you can introduce your students to the joy of throwing pots. For this you need clay and the following tools:

- Several sponges of different sizes to use when throwing on the wheel

- Plaster disks to place on the wheel head

- A needle tool for trimming the clay pot

- Different size tools for trimming and making a foot for the clay pot

- A wire tool for cutting the pot off the plaster disk

Make a list of students who would like to work on the wheel. Then schedule their time so that everyone has a chance. Remember that you/they will need at least 15 minutes to clean up the wheel.

For clay from failed pots, I suggest you get a 10-gallon plastic trash can with a lid and put some water in the bottom to keep the clay moist. When you need clay for the next day, just take out as much as you need and put it on a slab or disk of plaster before leaving school. The plaster will absorb the excess water, making the clay usable by the next day.

FIRING

As your students begin to finish their projects, you will need to start firing. First, locate three important areas near the kiln. One will be for greenware. Make a sign saying "Greenware—first firing" for that area. Then set aside space for "Bisque ware—second firing." Also make room for projects that have been fired and are to be returned, and make a sign for that area.

Two more signs near the kiln can be displayed as needed: "Firing greenware today" and "Firing bisque ware today." I tell the class beforehand which type of firing I will be doing that day and which the next.

Some rules and guidelines will help students get through the firing process smoothly. Here are mine:

1. Students are responsible for turning in the projects when they are ready to be fired. The projects should be turned in the day before the firing. Projects cannot be placed in the kiln after the firing has started.

2. All projects must be completely dry before they can be fired.

3. Sometimes you don't have room in the kiln for all the projects. Those that don't fit will be put in first for the next firing

4. Students should not handle others' objects, especially greenware.

5. Greenware and bisque ware cannot be fired together.

6. A firing takes 6 to 8 hours to heat the objects from room temperature to 1,800°F. Cooling down to room temperature then takes 10 to 12 hours.

7. All glazed projects must be dry-footed, meaning the bottom of the object can not be glazed. (optional)

8. I don't do ceramic firings on the weekend.

9. Students must check the firing area to see if their project has been fired.

I realize that for most art teachers who have trained in this area, these rules seem to be plain common sense. But I assure you that you will experience at least one of the following exchanges:

Student: When will the firing be finished?

Teacher: Around two o'clock.

Student: Well, can I come back later and get it, so I can give it to my mother today?

• • • • • •

Student: Why didn't you put my project in the kiln?

Teacher: I didn't have enough room. There is only so much room in the kiln.

Student: You can't stack the objects on top of each other?

Teacher: Yes, but only objects that are greenware.

Student: Well, my project is greenware. (The project is actually bisque ware.)

Teacher: But I'm firing bisque ware. (Teacher now tries to help student understand the difference between greenware and bisque ware. This may take several minutes.)

• • • • • •

Student: Are you going to be firing tomorrow?

Teacher: No, tomorrow is Saturday. Why do you ask?

Student: Well, I thought you would be doing firings on the weekend. Don't you have a key to the building?

Teacher: I have a key, but I also have other things planned for this weekend.

As you can see, ceramics lessons can be very demanding for an art teacher. If this is your first time teaching ceramics, I recommend you start with the basics. As your confidence increases over the years, expand the scope of your lessons. If you are an experienced art teacher, you can start with some of the more advanced techniques. The one thing to keep in mind is this: Don't take on more than you can handle. By keeping it simple, both you and your students can have a positive experience with clay. Students have a way of remembering your failures!

Working with Metal

I teach the metal foil process to my Art I and Art II students. It's a good medium for students who aren't proficient at painting or drawing; it gives them a feeling of artistic accomplishment.

Once you have chosen the classes in which you'll teach metals, you can plan your lesson and purchase supplies. You will need the following items:

- modeling tools

- tracer tools (pointed)

- spatula tools (flat)

- sheets or rolls of metal

- masking tape

- material to use as filler (acrylic modeling paste, plaster of paris, or instant papier-mâché)

- matting supplies

- paint to apply to the metal

- palette knives

- plastic molds for metal foil (optional)

If you have only one supply counter and shared trays, place one modeling tool, one tracer tool, and one spatula tool in each tray. Use colored tape to identify the different types of tools. Then student aides (who may not be from your art class) can easily tell if all tools have been included and returned.

Even if students have their own trays, it is probably too costly to purchase tools for each tray. Acquire enough tools for at least half of your largest class. Rarely is everyone working on the same step at the same time. Put one of each kind of tool in containers that you can keep an eye on and that students can get to easily.

As for the filler material, of the three kinds I mentioned above, I prefer instant papier-mâché. It is inexpensive and it doesn't dry out or harden if left uncovered for a while.

I buy a 5-pound bag when I'm ordering art supplies, and it usually lasts several years. In a 2-pound plastic margarine bowl, I mix enough papier-mâché to almost fill the bowl and place it on the supply counter along with two palette knives. I show students how to fill the cavity in their project, but they must do it themselves. Some complain; some have difficulty filling the cavity because they are using too much papier-mâché. But these are about the only problems I run into with this lesson.

Warn your students that the metal edges may cut them if they are not careful. They can place a piece of masking tape over the edges while they are working, and remove it when the project is matted. (See Mat Cutting, page 21.)

If you plan to use plastic molds, you should have several molds of each kind that you plan to work on so that students don't have to wait long for others to finish. Also, you or your aides must cut metal to the required size. I keep the cut metal in a tray on my desk so that I can see when I might need to have more cut and so that I can watch for metal being wasted.

You can keep the molds on the supply counter so that students can easily pick them up. Occasionally a mold will be put away in a supply tray or storage slot. Check for misplaced molds at the the end of the day.

If your students are creating their own metal designs, all you need is plenty of old newspaper. The tools would be set up in one of the ways described earlier.

Painting on Glass

Using small sheets of glass in the classroom is risky since there are so many chances for serious injury. Before you start the lesson, have a plan of action worked out with the school nurse in case of an injury. Also think about yourself. Most school systems require that all teachers have rubber gloves in case a student injury involves blood or other fluids. If your school system doesn't provide rubber gloves, buy them yourself.

Also require that each student have a liability waiver signed by a parent or guardian on file with you. A sample form is explained in Chapter 3 on page 42.

Once you have the above items, you may need to tell your students to bring a sheet of glass of a certain minimum and/or maximum size for this lesson. I tell my students that they can't use anything smaller than 8 inches by 10 inches or larger than 12 inches by 12 inches. Anything bigger would not fit into the 12-inch-wide slotted storage unit in our classroom.

Even if you ask students well in advance to bring their glass, you will still hear all kinds of excuses about why they didn't. So I do one simple thing. I call a local hardware store and get a price for an 8-inch by 10-inch sheet of glass. Then I take the names of the students who want me to buy the glass for them, and I collect their money. I call the hardware store before leaving school and order the glass I need. The next day at school, I use a china marker to write each student's name on the sheets of glass. I do not extend credit. If the student didn't pay when the glass was ordered, he or she must pay before receiving it.

Glass painting really requires no special tools. Students will have the brushes, paint tray, and water container that they need in their supply trays.

There are several ways to organize the glass paint. One would be to set out the colors in rows, and have students pick out the colors they need. Some students will pick up one of every color they need for their final design, even if they won't have time to use them all on the first day. That could cause a shortage. An alternative is to place one of each color on each group work table, in some kind of holder or plastic tray.

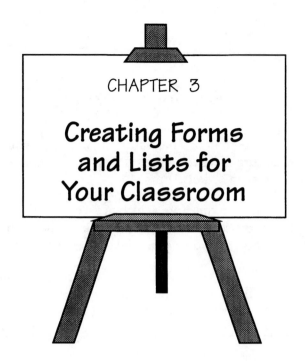

CHAPTER 3

Creating Forms and Lists for Your Classroom

During your teaching career you will probably draw up many forms and charts. In this chapter I describe those that I think are most commonly used in an art classroom. They include:

- a bell schedule for each period (so that you can allow for cleanup time)

- a list of classroom rules

- a sink cleanup schedule

- a teacher aide schedule

- a seating chart for each of your classes

- a master list for tray and slot assignments

- a tool sign-out form

- an insurance liability waiver

I hope my descriptions will help you draw up forms and lists that work for your specific needs.

Bell Schedule

If your school has more than one bell schedule, of course you'll have to make more than one chart. Be sure to leave enough time for cleanup in each period, so that each class can work in an orderly room.

I allow 15 minutes cleanup time for each class except for the last period, which gets 20. An accident or an extra large mess could make someone miss the bus, which you wouldn't want because then you might have to drive the student home yourself.

After a while, you will notice that students start cleaning up without being told. As they fall into a routine, the time spent on cleanup will decrease.

Sample Bell Schedule			
Period	Starts	Cleanup Time	Ends
1st	8:05	8:45	9:00
2nd	9:05	9:45	10:00
10:00–10:30—activity			
3rd	10:35	11:15	11:30
4th	11:35	12:15	12:30
12:30–12:55—lunch			
5th	1:00	1:40	1:55
6th	2:00	2:35	2:55

Post your bell chart near the clock. If you don't have a clock, get one. The chart and clock will save you from having to answer a lot of questions.

Some students try to take advantage of the cleanup time by using it for work for another class, or by saying 15 minutes beforehand that they don't want to start anything new because it's so close to cleanup time. This will happen regardless of the media your students are using. I've had students try this when we're using a pencil and ruler! Explain to the class that you're the one who'll decide when it's time to start cleaning up.

Classroom Rules

I recommend that you make a poster listing the rules of your classroom. Here are the areas you might want to cover:

1. *Seating Arrangement.* I use a seating chart throughout the school year, requesting that students sit at the same worktable every day. They may change chairs at that table, but they should stay at the same table. This helps me take roll very quickly, saving time for art lessons.

2. *Required Materials.* All of my students must have an art notebook. The notes for each lesson are written on the board, and students must copy them into their books. Each student must show the notes to me for a 100 daily grade. Students who don't copy the notes get a zero. I also require pencils for drawings. I will sell a pencil for 15 cents to any student who needs one. If a student doesn't have money and just wants to borrow a pencil, I ask for collateral—a pen, text-book, etc.—that I can hold until the pencil is turned in.

3. *Student Movement Within the Classroom.* I don't like students to wander around the room during class or after cleanup. When students enter my room, they are to sit down and to wait for class to start. After cleanup, students should be seated and wait for the bell to ring. Students are free to move around the classroom as needed during work periods, but they shouldn't wander around just because they have nothing else to do.

4. *Tool Breakage.* If a student accidently breaks a tool and comes to me and explains what happened, I will give the student a new tool and say nothing else about it. But if the student tries to hide the breakage and I find the broken tool later, I will ask the student to pay for it.

5. *Handling Others' Artwork.* I do not tolerate students handling others' work without permission. Sometimes they're just looking, but sometimes they're not.

6. *Throwing Paper at the Trash Can.* It is tempting for students to throw paper at the trash cans or recycling barrels to see if they can get it in, or just because they're too lazy to get up. This is distracting, disrespectful, and messy. I post a large sign on the wall behind each trash can in my classroom: "Whoever throws paper at the trash can and misses must pick up eight pieces of paper or sweep the room during activity period."

7. *Responsibility for Tools.* My students are responsible for all of the tools and materials that they use. The student who signs out a tool is responsible for bringing it back, even if another student at the table uses it. Accountability reduces tool loss and breakage.

8. *Artwork Turned in Late.* I deduct 10 points per day from the grade on any project turned in late. Students with excused absences are allowed extra time.

9. *Student Discipline.* I try to resolve discipline problems in the classroom. Sometimes, though, I have to send a student to the office. You must come up with your own guidelines about when to do this (unless your school has given you clear guidelines). Make it clear to students what your limits are. Try to be consistent in following your own guidelines.

10. *Art Fees.* Each student enrolled in an art class at my school has to pay a fee. The school board established this policy to help defray the cost of the art program. These fees usually give me a consistent budget. Make sure students understand how the art fee is collected and used. Occasionally, I have also received money from the principal's budget.

11. *My Desk.* The units that I use as a desk don't look like a typical teacher's desk. But my desk has the same restrictions. My desk is off limits to all students. Generally, there is nothing in my desk that is expensive or extremely important, but it's still my desk.

12. *Supply and Storage Cabinets.* The cabinets in my classroom are off limits to all students. My aides and I set out all supplies that students will need for any particular lesson. Students who want to use a tool other than what is provided in their tray may bring it in to class.

Some of these rules may make it seem like I'm being unduly harsh or suspicious. But over the years in my classroom, I've learned what works to maintain order and save money so that students can get the most from my classes and enjoy the creative experience.

Sink Cleanup Schedule

Students may be great about cleaning up their own tools and trays after a painting lesson. But what about the mess left in the sink? My pleadings fell on deaf ears until I hit upon a simple solution. Many times I had heard students complaining that washing out their paint trays was like doing dishes at home. The light dawned. I came up with a schedule in which everyone takes turns washing out the sink after the class cleans off the tools.

I assign two students per class per week to clean up the sink area, and I post the schedule above the sink in my room. If one student is absent, I still have someone. Or the two students may decide to take turns during the week. The schedule is made out for the entire school year. If some students drop or add the class, I drop them from or add them to the schedule. Students can easily see when their week is coming. I don't always have to remind them every day, but usually do so, just to make sure the job gets done before the bell rings.

The form I use is on page 38. You would fill it out by writing in the weeks chronologically going down the first column, then moving up to the top of the next column for the second turn of students 1 and 2, etc. Don't forget to skip vacation weeks when assigning turns.

Teacher Aide Schedule

If you decide to use student aides to hand out supply trays, you will probably need two per class (again, this allows for an absence). If students can earn credits as teacher aides in your school, so much the better. Use students you know or who are recommended by other teachers.

You may also be able to enlist aides from a study hall. Use them on a trial basis.

You can set up a student aide schedule like the sink cleanup schedule on page 38. I use the same form, except for the title at the top of the page. Make sure you don't write in people for sink duty and aide duty during the same week.

Some duties should probably *not* be assigned to your student aides. Those would include:

- taking the roll
- recording grades
- grading major tests
- averaging grades
- drawing up tests
- going into your purse, briefcase, or desk
- handling money

Sink Cleanup Schedule for _____ Period

Names	Week	Week	Week
1.			
2.	_____ - _____	_____ - _____	_____ - _____
3.			
4.	_____ - _____	_____ - _____	_____ - _____
5.			
6.	_____ - _____	_____ - _____	_____ - _____
7.			
8.	_____ - _____	_____ - _____	_____ - _____
9.			
10.	_____ - _____	_____ - _____	_____ - _____
11.			
12.	_____ - _____	_____ - _____	_____ - _____
13.			
14.	_____ - _____	_____ - _____	_____ - _____
15.			
16	_____ - _____	_____ - _____	_____ - _____
17.			
18.	_____ - _____	_____ - _____	_____ - _____
19.			
20.	_____ - _____	_____ - _____	_____ - _____

How to Organize and Manage Your Art Room

Seating Chart

Seating charts are important for a number of reasons. First, they help you learn students' names in each class. Second, and important for an art class, you can tell who did not clean up a certain table area after the lesson. Third, you can reassign seats to break up overly talkative or disruptive groups. And finally, you can take the roll at the beginning of class much more quickly and without having to call out every student's name.

I have a drawing for the arrangement of the tables in my room. I write each student's name and grade level on the appropriate table. I include the grade level because sometimes a whole class (9th, 10th, 11th, or 12th) may be called for an assembly and I can quickly verify the grade level of those who are leaving the room.

As I mentioned earlier, I don't really mind if students switch chairs at their table once the work begins. I also sometimes change the arrangement to break the monotony during the school year.

I place each seating arrangement in a plastic protective envelope, which goes into a binder. I lay the binder open to the page for the current class. After the tardy bell has rung, I use a china marker or washable felt-tip pen to mark A for absent or T for tardy, as appropriate. Later, I transfer those marks to my roll book.

Master List for Tray and Slot Assignment

With this form, you can quickly check to see which student has been assigned to a particular storage slot or supply tray. On a sheet of paper, you simply list the numbers of all the slots and supply trays you have assigned, with the students' names next to them.

If some students drop the the class during the school year, just remove their names from the list. When you get new students, assign them to the open tray and slot.

Assign trays and slots starting with the first class of the day and ending with the last. In this way, you have each class grouped together.

If you have only one supply counter, there may be some crowding when students pick up their trays at the beginning of each class. If you have a small room and this is a real problem, you could have your aides deliver the trays to the students, or designate one student from each work table to do so.

If you have two supply counters, put them in two different areas and divide your class into two sections.

Tool Sign-out Sheet

A sign-out sheet is a library system for your special tools and materials. You would use it whenever a student needs something that is not normally in the supply tray, such as ink bottles, lettering pens, a mat knife, small or large paintbrushes, or a carving tool.

The students simply write their names and the name of the tool on the sign-out sheet when taking something. Then they cross off their names when they bring it back. I keep the sign-out sheet on a clipboard near the tools.

I rely on the honor system 90 percent of the time. Sometimes I'll take the sign-out sheet around the classroom with me to see who has signed out a tool and who has not. I give a warning the first time a student fails to sign out a tool. The second time, I deduct 10 points from his or her daily grade. I rarely have to do this, however.

A sample sign-out sheet appears on page 41.

Insurance Liability Waiver

Some art techniques carry a risk of injury. I always give students a letter that they must have parents or guardians sign and that they must return to me before I will allow them to participate in any activity that might injure them.

The letter asks parents to state whether they have insurance that covers the child or whether they wish to sign up for our school insurance. Then, if a student does receive an injury that requires medical attention, I know that he or she has coverage and that the school and I are also protected. Also, the letter lets parents know that their son or daughter could receive a minor injury in the art program. They may inform you of any medical condition, such as hemophilia, HIV, or AIDS, that may affect handling and treatment of their child.

On page 42 is a sample insurance liability letter that you may copy or use as a model. You should probably run it by your principal before distributing it.

The top three lines are for your school name and address. Put your name after "From."

Sample Tool Sign-out Sheet

Name	Tool	Name	Tool

Sample Insurance Liability Letter

_____

_____

_____

From: _____

Re: School insurance

Student's name: _____

Dear Parent,

All students who participate in the school art program must be enrolled in a hospitalization plan. This school must have a letter from all parents or guardians stating that either their child is covered by such insurance or that they will subscribe to the school's insurance program.

    This school is not liable for injuries received by a student who is enrolled in the art program. Please complete and sign either Part 1 or Part 2 below and have your child return the letter to the school.

1. My son/daughter has adequate hospitalization insurance to participate in the art program at _____ ,
   name of school
   and I do not desire school insurance. I understand that the school is not liable for any injury that my son/daughter may receive.

   _____
   signature of parent or guardian

   _____
   date

2. I desire school insurance for my son/daughter so that he/she may participate in the art program at _____ .
   name of school
   I am sending $_____ in payment for our part of the school insurance. I request that the school pay its portion to cover my son/daughter.

   _____
   signature of parent or guardian

   _____
   date

Thank you for your cooperation in this matter.

    Sincerely,

_____
Art Teacher

CHAPTER 4

Worksheets, Forms, and Hints for Basic Art Lessons

I hope that the worksheets and ideas in this chapter will help you organize some basic art lessons so that all your students can reach the objectives you set.

The basic areas I cover here are:

- the color wheel
- linear perspective
- art appreciation
- watercolors
- ceramic casting
- elements of design
- putting together your own introductory material

This chapter does *not* include specific lesson notes, required readings, audio-visual requirements, teacher demonstrations, or suggestions for a specific curriculum. My aim is to give you information and worksheets that will help you organize or present your own lessons.

The reproducible worksheets in this chapter are very basic in design and objective. But using them gives me five benefits:

1. They set an objective for the student.

2. The student understands what must be done to achieve the objective.

3. The worksheets allow for the varying levels of artistic ability within a class.

4. They save explanation time, so you can spend more time with individual students.

5. They're easy to grade.

The Color Wheel

Most art teachers agree that students should study color theory. A good background will help them use color more effectively in their own work. I have always taught the color wheel and related color concepts, but the method I use today is different from the one I used at the start of my career.

I used to ask students to design their own layouts of the seven parts of the lesson:

1. color wheel

2. tints, shades, and tones

3. four basic color schemes

4. seven-step value scale

5. color intensity

6. warm colors

7. cool colors

Having students make up their own charts caused quite a few problems. Often, they would make a mistake in the layout and have to start over. Because each student's design was different, grading the sheets took me a long time. And sometimes, it was hard for me to determine if a student was missing a part of the lesson.

I didn't change my method for a while, though, because paper was plentiful. Then came the paper shortage of the mid-1970's. Normally, my students used 60- or 80-pound all-media paper for the color wheel lesson. I decided I would develop a standard design layout for each part of the lesson and then duplicate them on copy paper for each student.

I wasn't sure how copy paper would hold up to paint, so I tried some samples with tempera. The results were acceptable to me, and the paper also worked well with students wielding the paintbrush.

These standardized worksheets have resulted in several planned and unplanned benefits, including:

• The use of all-media art paper has decreased considerably.

• The completed work is easier and faster to grade.

- Students can easily determine which part of the lesson they must complete next. This gives me more time to help those who are having a problem.

- I no longer have to demonstrate how to lay out the charts to each class. I must only show what must be done to complete each part.

- Since I no longer have to give detailed demonstrations and layout information, students have more on-task time during the lesson.

On the following pages are samples of the seven worksheets that I use to organize the color wheel lesson. You may copy or adapt them for your own classes.

Once you have made enough copies of each worksheet, set out the seven stacks of worksheets on a table. Then students can progress at their own pace.

Sometime prior to the lesson, complete a set of worksheets so students can see what the finished product should look like. I make two sets and post one at the front of the room and one at the back.

Also prior to the lesson, you must consider what information you will give your students about the color wheel, and how you will present it.

I've found several options:

1. Give students a handout you have created with the information about the lesson.

2. Require the class to take notes during your presentation.

3. Put the information on the chalkboard for the students to copy into their notebooks.

4. Leave notes on the chalkboard until everyone has completed the entire lesson.

Color Theory Part 1:
A Color Wheel

Using only the three primary colors, red, yellow, and blue, mix the complete color wheel shown below. (Use prepared paint for white, black, and gray). The formulas for the secondary colors and intermediate colors are listed below the diagram.

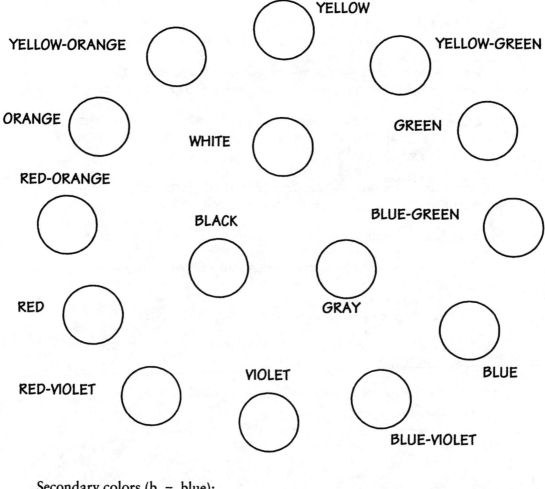

Secondary colors (b = blue):

r + y = orange   r + b = violet   y + b = green

Intermediate colors (b = blue, g = green):

r + o = r–o   y + o = y–o   r + v = r–v

b + v = b–v   b + g = b–g   y + g = y–g

Color Theory Part 2: Color Tints, Shades, and Tones

Make a tint, a shade, and a tone for the colors listed down the left side of the page.

Color	Tint	Shade	Tone
yellow			
y-orange			
orange			
r-orange			
red			
r-violet			
violet			
b-violet			
blue			
b-green			
green			
y-green			

Name _____   Period _____   Slot No. _____

Color Theory Part 3:
Four Basic Color Schemes

Complete each color scheme below with the correct colors. Be sure to *label* each color that you use.

Analogous Colors are next to each other on the color wheel.

1. _____

2. _____

3. _____

4. _____

Monochromatic Colors are made by using one color plus tints, shades, and tones of that same color.

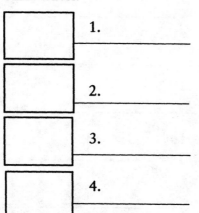

3 tints	3 shades	3 tones
light	dark	gray
lighter	darker	grayer
lightest	darkest	grayest

Complementary Colors are those opposite each other on the color wheel.

1. _____

2. _____

3. _____

4. _____

Triadic Colors are any three colors that are at an equal distance from each other on the color wheel.

1. _____

2. _____   3. _____

Color Theory Part 4:
A Seven-Step Value Scale

Using only black and white, create a seven-step value scale. Paint white in the first square. Then create a very light gray in your paint tray with a small amount of white and very small amount of black. Put this gray in the second square. Then add that same very small amount of black to the gray again and again to create darker grays as you go down the scale.

1.   **WHITE**

2.

3.

4.   **GRAY**

5.

6.

7.   **BLACK**

Color Theory Part 5:
Color Intensity

You can reduce the intensity of a color by mixing it with its complement. Mix the complementary colors below, using the ratio given in each square.

Example: For the first square below the all-yellow square, mix three brushfuls of yellow with one brushful of violet. Then paint the color in that square.

yellow

3Y
1V

2Y
2V

1Y
3V

violet

orange

3O
1B

2O
2B

1O
3B

blue

Color Theory Part 6:
Cool Colors

The colors on the wheel can be divided into two categories. We call the blues and greens *cool colors* because they suggest coolness. We call the reds and yellows *warm colors* because they suggest warmth.

Cool colors: green, blue-green, blue, blue-violet, violet
Warm colors: yellow, yellow-orange, orange, red-orange, red

Paint the design below with cool colors. You may make a tint, tone, or shade of any cool color you wish. Paint *all* parts of the design.

List the colors that you used: _____

_____

_____

_____

Color Theory Part 7:
Warm Colors

The colors on the wheel can be divided into two categories. We call the blues and greens *cool colors* because they suggest coolness. We call the reds and yellows *warm colors* because they suggest warmth.

Cool colors: green, blue-green, blue, blue-violet, violet
Warm colors: yellow, yellow-orange, orange, red-orange, red

Paint the design below with warm colors. You may make a tint, tone, or shade of any warm color you wish. Paint *all* parts of the design.

List the colors that you used: _____

_____

_____

_____

Linear Perspective

I didn't learn the concept of linear perspective until my first year in college. The instructor took us outside and had us sit down facing one of the campus buildings. Then he simply told us to draw that building using linear perspective. We all sat there looking at each other with our mouths hanging open! Only two of us knew what the instructor was talking about.

After many attempts, I began to understand perspective. As my understanding increased, I noticed that my artwork improved. It became clear to me that linear perspective would be an important part of any art curriculum.

You can buy lots of publications about perspective, but most of them have some shortcomings. The method may be confusing for beginners, or the terminology may be different from one author to another.

I teach perspective at three levels for my students:

1. First-year students use perspective to draw their own versions of cityscapes that I have created.

2. Second-year students draw their own versions of various houses I have designed.

3. Third-year students draw what they are actually seeing using one-point linear perspective.

For many years I showed students perspective drawings on transparencies and explained the cityscape or house that was on the screen. Sometimes I would go to the board and demonstrate how to draw a certain building or part. Yet students were still having great difficulty understanding perspective.

One year, I couldn't get an overhead projector from the media center for my Art I class, and I was forced to find another way to teach. That's when I started making my own drawings and having students copy them. I asked students to use either one-point or two-point linear perspective. The drawings were numbered so that I could quickly tell if students were missing any work.

I knew that tracing might be a problem, so I added a few conditions to the exercises. I gave students a sheet of paper that was larger than the original, and I required them to put their vanishing points on the horizon line at the edge of their paper. At other times, I asked them to make their drawings 25 percent smaller than the original.

At first, some students still didn't think I could tell if a drawing had been traced, but after I returned several traced drawings with a grade of zero, the tracing stopped.

After the Art I students draw a required number of cityscapes, they can design their own in either one-point or two-point linear perspective. On the board I list the required elements for the drawing—how many buildings, streets, parking lots, and so on. Each student does a preliminary drawing that I check for the required items. I give bonus points for things like air-conditioning units, park benches, extra windows, a billboard, etc.

Then the students get a 12- by 18-inch sheet and draw their final version, using colored pencils to finish it off.

ART II

I decided to try the same technique in my Art II classes, with houses as the subject instead of cityscapes. Using the same procedure as above, students copy drawings of houses. Then each student designs the floor plan of a house he or she would like to build, at a scale of $\frac{1}{4}$ inch = 1 foot.

Next, they each draw a two-point linear perspective illustration of the front and one side of the house. All windows, doors, and so on must be drawn according to their location in the floor plan. The students must also add some landscaping to the grounds.

Finally, the students draw the room that they would enter as they come into the house, using one-point perspective. This room should include everything that would be visible to someone entering it.

As a roundup, each student figures the square footage of the home and then the approximate cost. This puts it all in the proper "perspective."

ART III

Advanced students apply their knowledge of perspective to drawing a one-point linear perspective scene from life.

Usually, I divide the class into two groups. One group starts by drawing the art classroom, and the other draws the hallway outside the classroom. Then they switch.

I also review what they learned in Art II by having them draw several room interiors from copies. The rooms must contain all the necessary furniture, windows, doors, etc.

On the next three pages you'll find three perspective drawings that you can copy and use for this lesson.

Linear Perspective 1: Cityscape

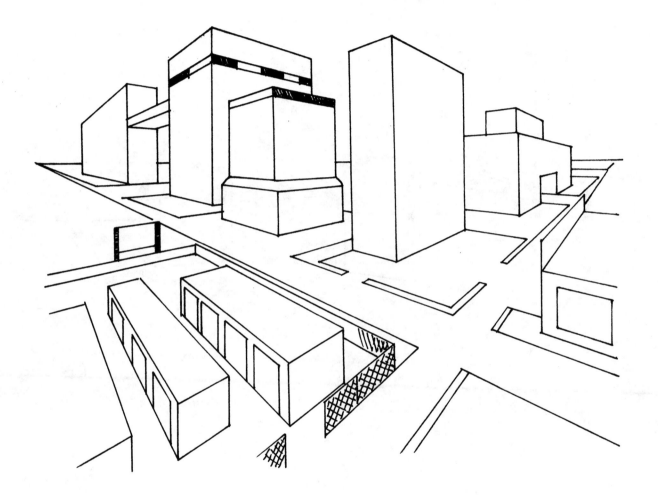

Linear Perspective 2: House

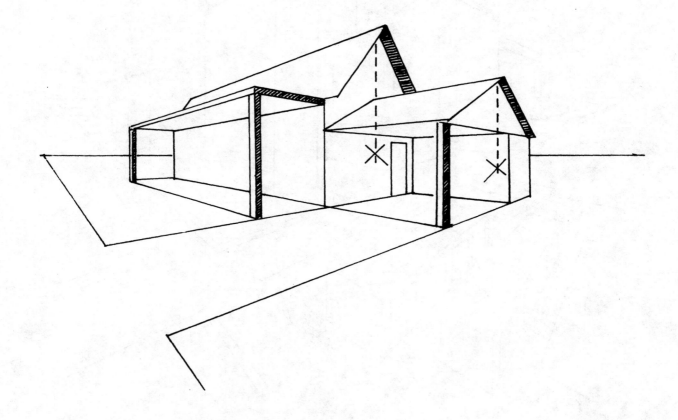

Linear Perspective 3: Interior

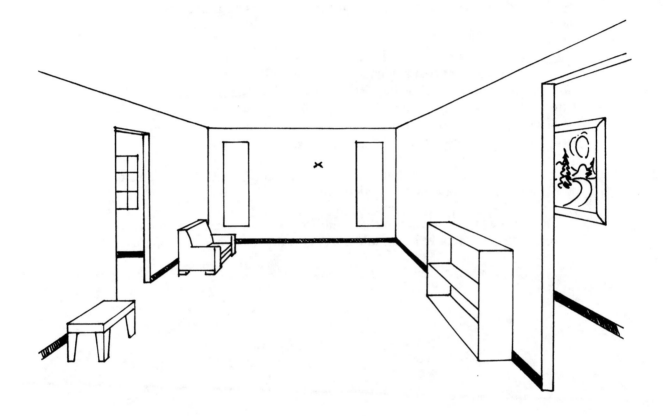

Ceramic Casting

I use only one sign-up sheet for ceramic casting. On it, students list which molds they would like to use. This helps me organize the lesson. I can choose the students who will be casting the next day, determine which molds must be set out for them, and quickly see which students have made their first casting and which have not.

After each student has made the first casting, I no longer need the forms. In my classes, I don't require that students make any additional castings. However, students may make more castings if they want, and a majority choose to do so. I charge 50 cents for each additional casting to help pay for the slip and glaze, and I collect it at the time of the casting. I don't extend credit because I don't want to get into complicated record keeping for these fees.

If some students don't plan to make additional castings, they will have to have something else to work on during that time.

On the next page is a form that students can use to list their preferences for molds. Remember to give each mold a name so that everyone can refer to it easily.

Name _____ Period _____ Slot No. _____

Ceramic Casting Preferences

In the spaces below, please list the molds that you would like to cast during this lesson. Every attempt will be made to give you your first choice. However, you may have to cast your second or third choice if too many people want to make the same thing.

Only your first casting will be graded. Any additional castings that you do for fun will not be. The cost of additional castings is $ _____ each. We will use this money to buy additional supplies.

Choice	Mold Name	Date Cast
1st		
2nd		
3rd		
4th		

Art Appreciation

As art teachers, we would like to think that art students are naturally interested in art history and appreciation. The awful truth is that many are bored with it until they begin to have more of their own experiences with art. If you have not had much success teaching art appreciation, you're not alone.

When I first started teaching, I was naive enough to think that students would pay attention to films or slides if I asked them to. Usually, however, half the class would be asleep within the first 20 minutes. I made various threats about having them take notes or giving them a test about the program, to little avail.

Attempts at class discussions were also usually a bust. Students who did participate made inappropriate statements or asked unrelated questions. I'm not telling you this to discourage you, just to prepare you. It may be that teaching art appreciation is your forte, and you may have greater success than I did.

I was just about to give up on art appreciation when I hit upon a new idea. I would give students worksheets to complete *while* they were watching a program. I still had some diehards, but after their worksheets were returned with zeros, they began to pay more attention.

Today I still try to have a discussion before an art appreciation program, but I keep it short. After the discussion I hand out the worksheet and make sure that every student can see the screen and is not being disturbed by someone else.

I create a worksheet by viewing the program beforehand and writing questions in the order in which the material appears. I design the questions so that students can answer them in just a few words. Difficult words that appear in the program are listed at the bottom of the sheet.

The worksheets increase the amount of material I must grade, but I have my aides check them first and circle any answers they're not sure of. Then I go over the worksheets and grade them.

If students are absent on the day the program is shown, I simply require that they write a two-page report on the same subject. Sometimes I can tell that they have just copied the information from the encyclopedia, but at least they did go over the material somehow.

Of course, slide and tape programs are not the only way to teach art appreciation. You can involve students by having them pick favorite works out of art books and tell why they like the works. You can have them try to create something in the style of a favorite artist. And you can take field trips to galleries and museums. Every class is different. Be prepared to try a variety of approaches before you hit on one that works.

Watercolors

Most art curriculums give students a chance to explore watercolors (aquarelles). I use this medium in my Art II classes. You could use a video to introduce techniques. But if your budget is limited, or if you are sufficiently confident in your own painting ability, you can simply demonstrate techniques yourself.

From the start of my teaching career, I would demonstrate the two basic techniques used in watercolors: drybrush and wet-on-wet. Occasionally I would finish a painting so that students could see the whole process.

Often, I felt there might be something missing from the lesson. The work my students were turning in was lacking in one or more of these areas:

- value changes

- shading and highlighting

- suggestive qualities (using color values)

- transparent qualities (taking advantage of the layering of colors possible in watercolor)

- the successful painting of plants and trees (using different greens and different brushes)

I decided to develop a series of worksheets that would give students a chance to practice in these areas before creating their own paintings. My students must complete each of these six worksheets before starting a composition on watercolor paper.

To prepare for the lesson, you should complete an example of each worksheet and hang the set where everyone can see it. Then copy the blank worksheets and lay out the six stacks in an accessible area so that students can work at their own pace.

The worksheets are numbered so that students can staple them together in order when they are finished. That enables you to determine quickly if a student has completed them all.

After my students finish the worksheets, I require them to make two watercolor paintings over the course of the rest of the unit. They may do the first painting on any subject matter they wish. They do the second from a still life I set up in the classroom.

On the next six pages are samples of the worksheets I use in my classroom. I hope they will work for you as well.

Watercolor Worksheet 1:
Value

Value means the relative lightness or darkness of colors or of areas in a painting. There are many different degrees of lightness or darkness found between white and black, or between white and a color.

DARK

Part 1. Use *one* color to create a value scale that goes from dark to light, just by gradually increasing the amount of water you add to a color. Start with very little water.

LIGHT

LIGHT

Part 2: Using *one* color and white watercolor paint, create a value scale from light to dark by gradually increasing the amount of color that you add to the white. Start with very little color.

DARK

Watercolor Worksheet 2:
Shading

Shading means (1) using color values to create a three-dimensional effect and (2) adding small amounts of black to a color to make it darker.

Part 1. Choose *one* color and shade the three objects below using different values of that color.

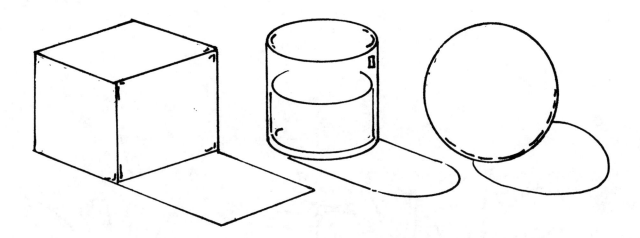

Part 2: Select *one* color and add small amounts of black to it to create shading for the objects below. Then use a light value of black for the shadows.

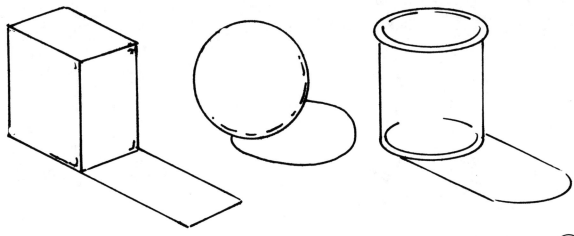

Watercolor Worksheet 3:
Foliage

Using different greens and different brushes, an artist can create the illusion of tree or plant foliage.

Create foliage for the trees below. Use a fan brush for one tree and a stiff bristle brush for the other.

 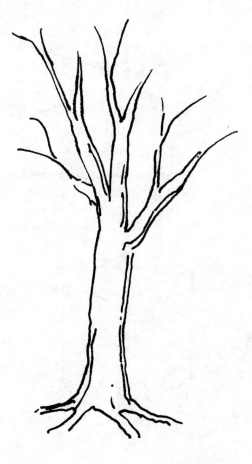

Watercolor Worksheet 4:
Transparency

Watercolor paint has a transparent quality. That allows you to create new colors by painting one color over another.

In each box below, paint one color over another as directed.

1. yellow over red	2. blue over yellow	3. red over blue
4. yellow over blue	5. red over yellow	6. blue over red

Watercolor Worksheet 5:
Highlighting

Highlighting is a technique for showing that light is bouncing off an object in the painting. In watercolor painting, you leave the paper white where you want highlights.

Use one color for each object below, and create a highlight on each by letting an area of the white paper show.

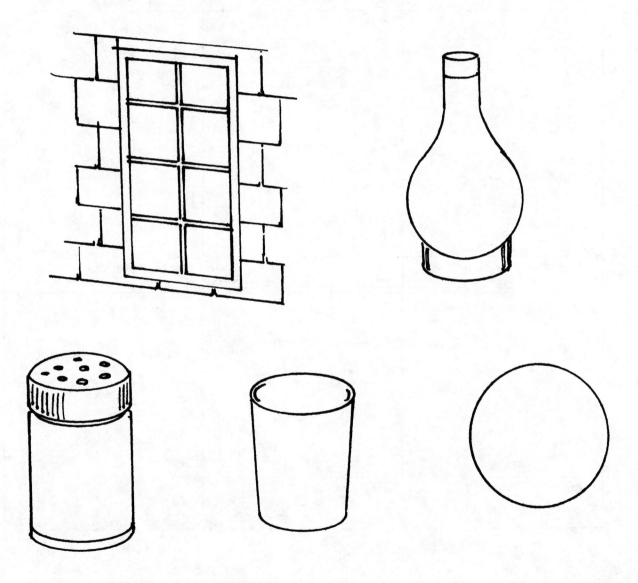

Watercolor Worksheet 6:
Suggestive Qualities

An artist can help create the illusion of distance (aerial perspective) with different values of watercolor.

Paint the scene below using different values of the colors you select to make it appear that the background is receding. You may not use plain black or add black to a color. Decide which direction the light in the scene is coming from before you begin.

How to Organize and Manage Your Art Room

The Elements of Design

Some concepts in art may be difficult for high school students to understand. The elements of design may be included in that category. Over the last 22 years, I have tried various methods for teaching design; the results have sometimes been disappointing, especially in my advanced classes. If students in those classes plan to go on to higher art education, a basic understanding of design will give them an edge.

When I had finished creating the watercolor worksheets, I realized a similar, very basic approach might work in presenting the elements of design. I developed simple worksheets for each element, and through doing them, my students did gain an improved understanding.

The basic elements I cover are:

- shape

- form

- value

- space—foreground and background; positive and negative; overlapping; convergence; size relationships

- line

- texture

Before starting your design classes, assemble a number of objects that students can draw one at a time and in arrangements, as required throughout these exercises. Those objects might include bottles, flasks, and vases; books; fruit; plates; mugs; boxes; and so on. Your classroom probably contains everything you might need. The worksheets that require objects or still lifes are:

Worksheet 3: Shape and Form, Part C—bottle

Worksheet 4: Shape and Form, Part D—complex object

Worksheet 5: Value, Part A—one object

Worksheet 6: Value, Part B—three objects

Worksheet 7: Value, Part C—two objects

Worksheet 8: Value, Part D—three objects

Worksheet 9: Space, Part A—three objects

Worksheet 13: Line, Part A—still life

Worksheet 15: Texture—object

Worksheet 16: Final Composition—still life

On the next sixteen pages are examples of the design worksheets I use.

You can also have students look at and talk about examples of good design, be it architectural, industrial, graphic, decorative, or fine art. Resource books abound, and design is all around us. Every manufactured or built object we use, touch, or look at, from a cereal box to a toothbrush to a button, has been designed by someone. Each designer probably started with a sketch, whether on paper or on a computer screen. If you can begin to open students' eyes to design in their lives, they may put forth more effort in class.

Name _____ Period _____ Slot No. _____

Elements of Design Worksheet 1:
Shape and Form, Part A

    A *shape* is an outlined area with length and width. It is two-dimensional (2D). The basic shapes are circle, square, rectangle, triangle, and free form (as found in nature).

    A *form* has, or appears to have, length, width, and depth. It is, or looks, three-dimensional (3D). Some basic forms are the cube, cone, cylinder, sphere, and free form.

    In 2D art, you can show form with shading, perspective, color, and so on. In Box 1 below, draw a vertical rectangle and then make it into a cylinder like the example. In Box 2, draw an object that is based on a cylinder and looks as though it has mass or is solid.

1. rectangle that becomes a cylinder	2. cylinder-based object
Example: a cylinder	*Example:* A fence post has mass and is solid

Name _____   Period _____   Slot No. _____

Elements of Design Worksheet 2:
Shape and Form, Part B

A cylindrical form that is *volumetric* is a cylinder that could hold something.
In Box 1 below, draw a vertical rectangle and then make it into a cylinder that
is volumetric. In Box 2, draw an everyday object that is cylindrical and volumetric.

1. cylinder that could hold something	2. everyday object that is cylindrical and volumetric
Example: cylinder that is volumetric	*Example:* A drainpipe

Elements of Design Worksheet 3:
Shape and Form, Part C

Complex shapes and forms: Most objects that are three-dimensional or look 3D are a combination of two or more shapes or forms. These objects are referred to as having complex shapes or forms.

    In Box 1, a cone has been drawn. In Box 2, draw your own cone. Shade it to make it appear 3D. In Box 3, draw the bottle on your table. Use the three steps shown below Box 3. Do *not* shade your completed drawing in Box 3.

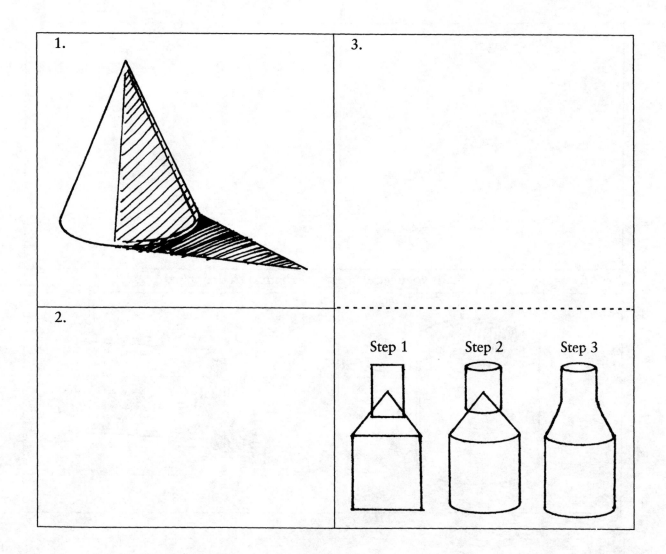

1.

3.

2.

Step 1   Step 2   Step 3

Name _____ Period _____ Slot No. _____

Elements of Design Worksheet 4:
Shape and Form, Part D

Complex shapes and forms: In Box 1, draw the object on your table using the three steps illustrated below. In Box 2, draw the second object placed on your table and answer the two questions.

1.	2.
Step 1 Step 2 Step 3	What shapes do you see in the object? _____ _____ _____ What forms do you see in the object? _____ _____ _____ _____

How to Organize and Manage Your Art Room

Elements of Design Worksheet 5:
Value, Part A

Values are the many different grays between black and white.

In Box 1, using the side of your pencil lead, create a 9-step value scale. In Box 2, shade the three objects with the side of your pencil so that each object has a *different* value. Do not create any shadows or highlights. In location D, draw your own object and give it a value.

1. 9-Step Value Scale

WHITE

BLACK

2. A. This object is red.

B. This object is light yellow.

C. This is light blue.

D.

What color is your object?

_____

How to Organize and Manage Your Art Room

Elements of Design Worksheet 6:
Value, Part B

With light values, you can create *highlights* on an object.
In Section 1 below, shade each object with the side of your pencil lead. Then erase a small area to create a highlight where light would be reflected off the object. In Section 2, draw three objects of your own and shade them with your pencil. Then create a highlight on each object.

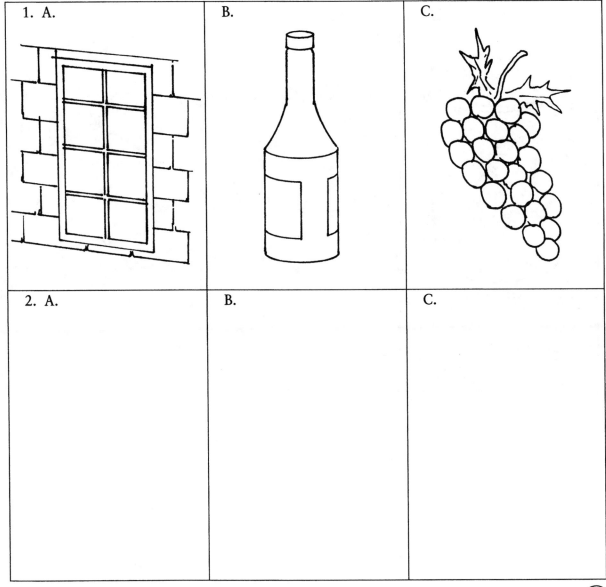

Name _____   Period _____   Slot No. _____

Elements of Design Worksheet 7:
Value, Part C

    With dark values, you can create *shadows* on an object and in the area around it.

    In Boxes 1 through 4, shade the whole object. Then create a shadow *on* the object and a shadow *cast by* the object. In Boxes 5 and 6, draw two more objects and shade them. Then create shadows on them and for them. Do *not* add highlights.

How to Organize and Manage Your Art Room

Elements of Design Worksheet 8:
Value, Part D

You can create a three-dimensional object by using many different values. With your pencil, draw the three objects arranged on the table. Shade each one so that it has the following: (1) a different value from the others, (2) highlights, (3) shadows on the object, and (4) a shadow on the table.

1.

Answer these questions while looking at your finished drawings.

1. Of the three objects you drew, which has the:

   lightest value? _____

   medium value? _____

   darkest value? _____

2. Which object has the:

   lightest shadow? _____

   medium shadow? _____

   darkest shadow? _____

Name _____ Period _____ Slot No. _____

Elements of Design Worksheet 9:
Space, Part A

Space is the occupied or unoccupied areas within a drawing or painting. (Occupied space is called *positive* space; unoccupied is called *negative*.) All space within a drawing or painting is said to be in one of these three areas: the *foreground*, which is the area nearest the viewer; the *middle ground*, which is farther back from the viewer; and the *background*, which is the area farthest from the viewer.

In the space below, draw the three objects arranged for you. Include highlights and shadows.

After your drawing is finished, answer these questions.

Which object is in the:

foreground? _____

middle ground? _____

background? _____

                       How to Organize and Manage Your Art Room

Elements of Design Worksheet 10:
Space, Part B

An artist can use three techniques to create the illusion of space in an artwork:
(1) *overlapping* of shapes or forms, (2) *convergence*, and (3) *size relationships*.
Overlapping means one shape or form extending over another. (We'll cover convergence and size relationships later.)

Using geometric shapes (squares, rectangles, circles, and triangles), draw a design that creates the illusion of space by overlapping shapes of similar size. Then color your design with colored pencils.

Elements of Design Worksheet 11:
Space, Part C

An artist can use *convergence* to create an illusion of space. In convergence, shapes or forms appear to move toward or meet at one point in space.

Using geometric shapes, create a design that makes it seem as if shapes or forms are moving toward or meeting at one point. You may use shapes or forms of different sizes. Then color your design with colored pencils.

Elements of Design Worksheet 12:
Space, Part D

An artist can use *size relationships* to create a sense of space in a painting or drawing. Smaller shapes appear to be farther away, and larger shapes appear to be closer to the viewer.

Using geometric shapes, create an illusion of space. *Don't* overlap the shapes or have them converge at one point.

81 *How to Organize and Manage Your Art Room*

Elements of Design Worksheet 13:
Line, Part A

A *line* may show direction or movement. A line defines a shape by showing its *contour*.

Select one of the arrangements set out for you. Draw only the contour, or outline, of the objects. You do not have to draw the table the objects are on.

Elements of Design Worksheet 14:
Line, Part B

Lines may show *direction* or *movement*.
Trace your drawing from Worksheet 13 onto this sheet. Then use lines that go around, up and down, across, or in other directions to create direction and motion.

Name _____ Period _____ Slot No. _____

Elements of Design Worksheet 15:
Texture

Texture is the quality of a surface—rough, smooth, sticky, furry, shiny, etc. With your pencil, create textures for the objects in 1–3. In Box 4, draw an object of your choosing and give it a texture. If you like, make it a texture we wouldn't expect that object to have.

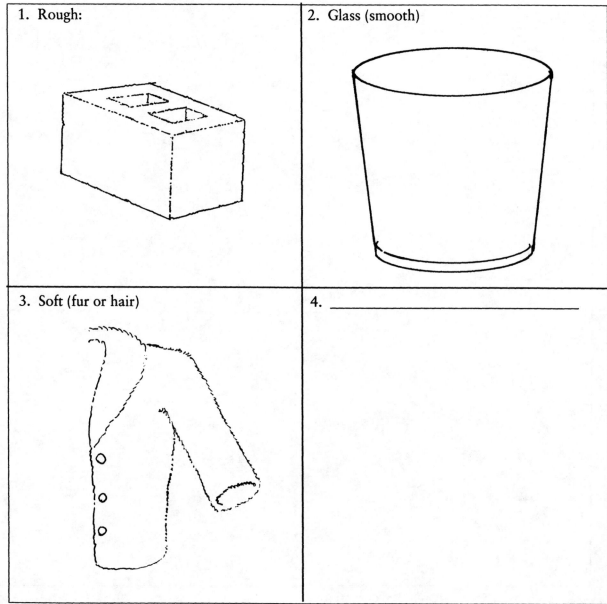

1. Rough:

2. Glass (smooth)

3. Soft (fur or hair)

4. _____

Elements of Design Worksheet 16:
Final Composition

Using all the concepts we have studied, draw an arrangement of objects in the space below.

Putting Together Introductory Material

Over the years I have developed a number of worksheets and homemade booklets for my students. You will, too. Why?

1. They provide background information and practice in the specific areas you want to emphasize.

2. They stress the importance of reading in art as well as in other areas.

3. They provide a way to keep students on task, instead of wasting class time.

4. They decrease discipline problems and confusion.

I'm always looking for material that I can use to create a worksheet or information booklet for a specific lesson in my curriculum. The worksheets contain questions that the student can answer while reading or art exercises that require no reading.

For information booklets, I use my college notes as well as notes I've taken while perusing art magazines and other periodicals and books. Creating my own booklets lets me give students the right amount of information for my lessons.

I've found that about 25 copies of each booklet is usually enough, along with worksheets for everyone in the class. I use the booklet to introduce the upcoming lesson. After finishing the current lesson, a student can get a booklet and start answering the questions on the accompanying worksheet.

As a rule, I start a new lesson when at least half the class has finished the current lesson. I don't like to waste fast students' class time by waiting for every student to finish.

I use the information booklets for:

- the color wheel

- linear perspective

- commercial art

- cartooning

- art appreciation

I use worksheets with art exercises (like those in this chapter) for:

- watercolors

- elements of design

And I use both information booklets and exercise worksheets for:

- the color wheel

- linear perspective

Another benefit of creating your own materials is that you can refresh your own memory and get new ideas for many different areas of art. This is sure to make you a better teacher than someone who uses the same ready-made materials year after year.

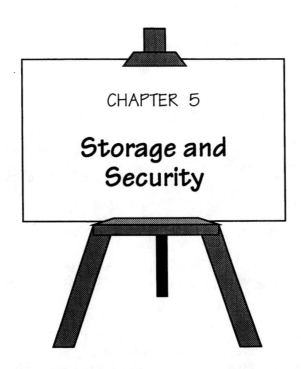

CHAPTER 5

Storage and Security

As a new teacher, you may be assigned to either of two kinds of art classrooms: a classroom designed for teaching art, or a regular classroom converted (or worse, temporarily designated) for art use.

I hope you have a room that was designed to have sufficient work space, storage space, and cleanup areas for the teaching and learning of art. My room has always been a dedicated art classroom. I have made some changes to the layout, but it is basically the same as it was in 1971.

Storage of Art Supplies

IN AN ORIGINAL ART CLASSROOM

Most college courses for art teachers don't touch on how to organize and store art materials. Simply putting materials into any available cabinet won't work. You would spend a lot of your school day looking for things you know you have "somewhere." When you come into a new classroom, time spent getting organized is well worth it.

I store my materials according to the lessons I have planned for the year. For example, here are the materials needed for linoleum block printing:

- linoleum blocks
- carving tools
- printing ink
- metal inking plates

- printing press (optional)
- hard rubber rollers
- print paper
- palette knives

I place all of these materials in one cabinet. The only material I might store separately would be the paper. Generally, I keep all types of paper in three large drawers that are part of my desk.

I recommend you make a list of the lessons you plan for the coming year. Then make a list of materials needed for each lesson. After you do these two things, take a look at the cabinet space you have. As a rule, I allow one cabinet for each major lesson such as linoleum block printing, ceramics, airbrush, tempera, and Plexiglas™ etching. I only need half a cabinet for each of these lessons: screen printing, enameling, metal foil, macramé, rug making, pastels, and watercolors.

You don't have to keep everything in the same cabinet year after year. Every school year I have to move some materials for one reason or another.

If you have materials that you use in more than one lesson (and who doesn't?), you can still be organized. This group of multipurpose materials might include rulers, brushes, paint trays, compasses, pencils, mat knives, erasers, etc. I store all brushes and trays in one cabinet. I store rulers in the same drawers as the art paper. I put pencils and erasers in the cabinet with pastels and watercolor sets.

Some materials don't have to take up cabinet space because you can easily and cheaply replace them if they are taken or damaged. They might include polystyrene wig heads, cardboard for T-shirt painting, various objects for still-life drawing, and so on.

I recommend that after finishing a lesson, you always have students clean up tools and materials before putting them away. If something is broken, you can repair it or put it on the list of items to purchase. In this way, you're always ready for the next time you need those items.

IN A CONVERTED ART CLASSROOM

If enough cabinets were built when the classroom was converted, you don't have a problem. If you don't have enough cabinets, you may be able to get the industrial arts teacher and students to build some as a class project. Or, you could undertake the construction yourself!

I have often relied on the shop teacher in my school. Generally, I have purchased the materials from my art budget, and the shop teacher has overseen the construction. There have been times when I've had to construct the item I needed. If you can't or won't divide your time between instruction and construction, you may have to come in early, stay late, or work on weekends to get your project done.

If it is possible to do construction during class time, you can take the opportunity to have interested students put their skills to good use. Be aware that some students have excellent intentions but lack the coordination to hammer a nail in straight.

One more source of help might be your school custodian. Years ago I wanted to add another sink. I had requested one from the school each year, but I was always told there wasn't enough money, and besides, what did I need another sink for? I already had one.

The problem was, with one sink I had to allow 20 minutes for 30 students to clean up, which seriously cut into productive class time. Finally, my principal agreed to pay for the plumbing for a new sink, but he would not send in a work order for it to be installed. Installation, under our agreement, would be my job. I guess he figured I wasn't capable of putting in a sink, because he had the biggest grin across his face when he said yes to the plumbing.

The last laugh was mine, however, because I had already talked to the custodian about how to do the plumbing. He told me what I needed and how to put it together. He also volunteered to help if I ran into any problems. I put a sign in the teacher lounge letting everyone know I was looking for a used sink. Later that same day, the band assistant told me he had just replaced his old sink and I could have it if I wanted it.

Installing the sink took me several weeks, but it was worth it, especially for the look on my principal's face when I handed him the charge slips for the various plumbing supplies I had purchased. The moral of the story is, don't overlook the custodian as a source of help.

If you need more storage space and you really can't build it for some reason, there may be small storage rooms elsewhere in the school, such as in the industrial arts department, that you could use. Before you start a lesson, you should make a list of all the materials you need and retrieve them from the storage room. If you go this route, a utility cart or child's wagon could help you bring everything along.

It may take several years for you to get your art classroom the way you really want it. I recommend that you make a list of your requirements and prioritize them. Then get to work on the first thing on your list!

Protecting Against Theft and Misuse

Before I first started teaching in 1971, none of my professors had mentioned that theft of art materials might be a problem. I was naive enough to think that no one would take anything that didn't belong to him (or her) over the summer or during holidays. I was in for a big surprise.

When someone stole $200 worth of art materials (in 1973 dollars), I thought my principal would give me the money to replace those supplies. Instead, the principal said I would have to use the art fee money to replace the materials. Back then, students paid $2 each to take an art course. (Today the fee is $12.) But in 1973, $2 was a significant amount of money for most students and their parents. I asked the principal about the school district's insurance for theft and was shocked to learn that only the office and library were covered.

I decided after this incident that I would buy some padlocks for each cabinet. The previous art teacher had installed a hasp with a padlock on each cabinet, but during the first year I had to remove them because most of the keys or padlocks were missing.

Basically, any lock with a larger-than-normal shackle will work on a pair of doors with handles that are close together (see illustration).

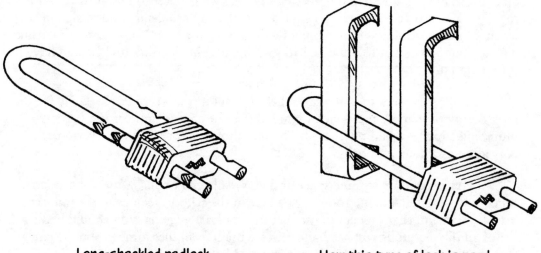

Long-shackled padlock
(e.g., bicycle lock)

How this type of lock is used
with a cabinet

A majority of the cabinets in my classroom are like this. If your cabinets have knobs instead of handles, you can replace them quite cheaply so that you can add padlocks.

I have numbered each cabinet and put the same number on each corresponding key and lock.

Some cabinets in my room are different from those shown on the previous page. I also have some drawers in which I store art papers. For a long time, all I did was hammer some nails into these drawers and cabinets at the end of each year. Anyone with enough strength or a crowbar could pull them open. This did happen a few times and I lost some materials.

Finally I decided to try something a little more sophisticated. What I finally came up with works exactly as I hoped it would. This arrangement calls for one screw eyelet, and two bolt eyelets with nuts. The drawing below shows how this lock-holder is installed.

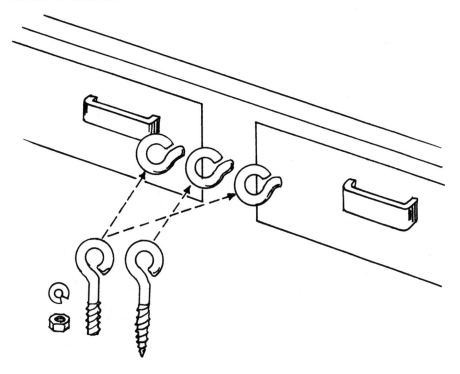

A lock for two adjacent drawers

Screw a bolt eyelet into each drawer as shown, and secure it with a nut on the inside of the drawer. Put the screw eyelet into the middle piece of the desk. Now you have three eyelets lined up, through which you can put a long-shackled padlock.

Of course, we all know that if someone really wants to steal something or cause you distress, a padlock is not going to stop that person. But these locks will deter a lot of casual, opportunistic theft, as well as the temptation for students to "borrow" supplies that they might neglect to return.

LOCKING YOUR KILN

Another thing you might consider putting a lock on is your kiln. I never really gave it much thought until one time when I was absent and the substitute apparently was asleep at the wheel. He allowed the students to do what they wanted while he spent the day talking to his girlfriend, who came to school with him!

Two students thought it would be exciting to put a bottle of white glue in the kiln. Needless to say, the glue and its container melted, creating a unique design inside the kiln. The only way I could get it out was to do a firing with nothing else in the kiln. It created a smell I'll never forget.

If you do put a lock on your kiln, you must choose an area in which a screw will not make contact with an element. If a screw touches an element, it will heat up whenever the kiln does, creating the potential for a burn. Also take care when drilling holes for the screws that you do not damage an element.

CHAPTER 6

Construction Plans

Here are some simple construction plans for the items I discussed in Chapter 1. I hope these inventions work as well for you as they have for me.

The Supply Counter

The supply counter (Chapter 1, page 2) is constructed with the following materials:

5 sheets of $\frac{1}{2}$" plywood sanded on one side
two 2 x 4's (2" x 4" x 96")
2 pounds of finishing nails
$\frac{1}{2}$ pound of 2" nails

Cut the plywood so that you have the following sizes to use:

2 pieces – 18" x 95" x $\frac{1}{2}$ " (A)   1 piece – 38" x 96" x $\frac{1}{2}$ " (D)

27 pieces – 12" x 12" x $\frac{1}{2}$ " (B)   2 pieces – 18" x 37" x $\frac{1}{2}$ " (E)

2 pieces – 18" x 96" x $\frac{1}{2}$ " (C)   30 pieces – 9" x 12" x $\frac{1}{2}$ " (F)

On page 98 is the layout for cutting each sheet of plywood to obtain the pieces listed above. If you're doing this yourself, set your skill saw so that it will cut $\frac{1}{2}$" plywood. Remember to use safety glasses, and don't do this while you are alone in the school, or during school hours.

After you have built this supply counter, you will have some wood left over. Save it for a future project.

SUPPLY COUNTER: DIRECTIONS FOR ASSEMBLY

See illustrations on the following pages for help.

1. Nail the two end pieces (18" x 37") to the top and bottom panels (18" x 96"). Setting them on the floor makes it easier.

2. Measure down 12" from the inside of the top panel on one side panel and mark that location.

3. Repeat step 2 on the other side panel.

4. Take one of the 18" x 95" pieces and nail in place, so that the top edge of the piece is on your mark.

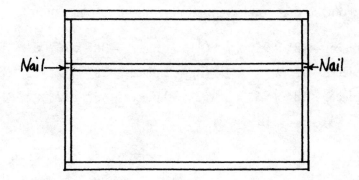

5. Measure down 12" from the bottom of the piece you installed in step 4 and mark that location on each side panel.

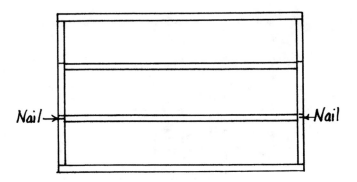

6. Take the remaining 18" x 95" piece and nail in place, again setting the top edge of the piece on your mark.

7. Cut the 2 x 4's so that you have four pieces measuring 32" x 2" x 4" and four pieces measuring 18" x 2" x 4". These will form the legs of the supply counter. See page 100.

8. Nail the two leg sections to the bottom of the supply counter.

9. Start nailing together the pieces of wood that form each cubbyhole. Nail a 9" x 12" piece to the middle of a of a 12" x 12" piece as shown on page 101. These pieces will form two cubbyholes when nailed into the supply counter. Do that by driving the nail diagonally into the wood. There will be a small amount of unused space at the end of each section of cubbyholes.

10. Nail on the back panel (38" x 96"). Now you're ready to paint the counter.

Supply Counter 1:
Cutting the Five Sheets of Plywood

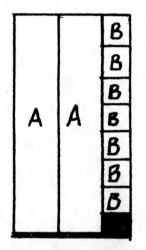

2 – 18" x 95" (A)
7 – 12" x 12" (B)

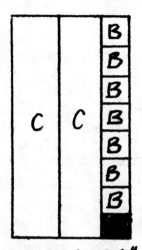

2 – 18" x 96" (C)
7 – 12" x 12" (B)

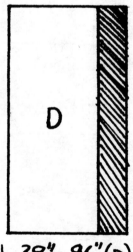

1 – 38" x 96" (D)

2 – 18" x 37" (E)
12 – 12" x 12" (B)
7 – 9" x 12" (F)

23 – 9" x 12" (F)
1 – 12" x 12" (B)

 Extra wood pieces

Note: Not drawn to correct proportions.

Supply Counter 2:
Nailing Together the Sides, Top,
Bottom, and Middle Sections

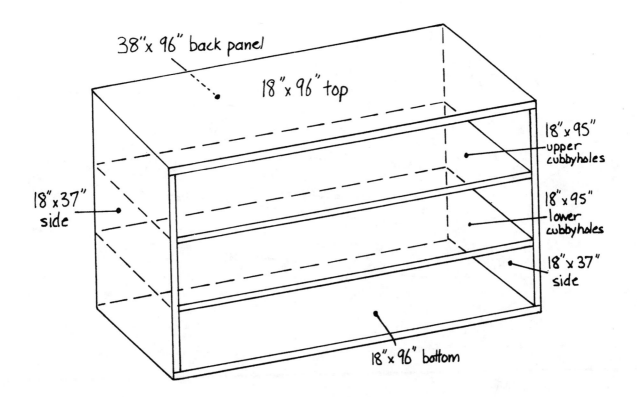

38"x 96" back panel

18"x 96" top

18"x 95" upper cubbyholes

18"x 37" side

18"x 95" lower cubbyholes

18"x 37" side

18"x 96" bottom

Supply Counter 3:
Cutting and Nailing Together
the Pieces for the Leg Sections

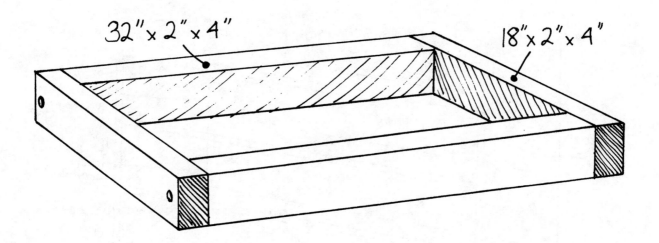

Supply Counter 4:
Nailing Together the Pieces That
Form the Rows of Cubbyholes

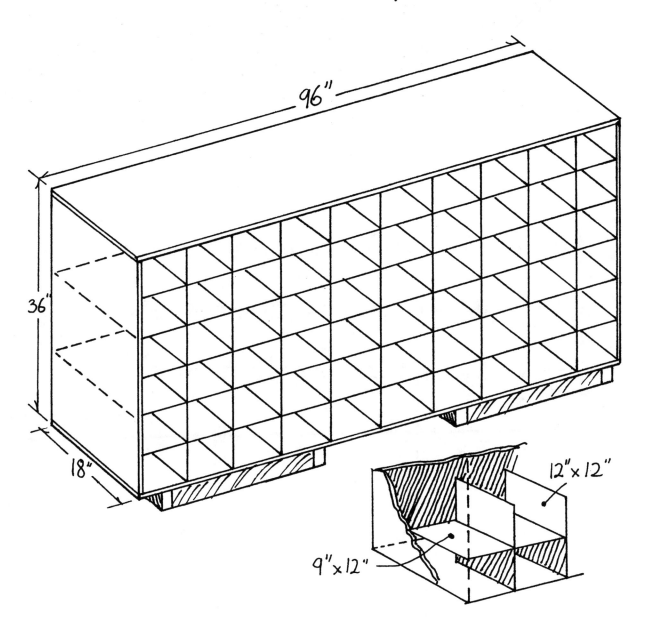

Slotted Storage Unit

To build a slotted storage unit like the one discussed in Chapter 1 (pages 6 and 7), you will need:

> 2 sheets of $\frac{1}{2}$" plywood
> 1 pound of $1\frac{1}{2}$" finishing nails

Cut the plywood so that you have the following pieces for at least one storage unit (you will have some wood left over):

> 21 pieces – 12" x 16" x $\frac{1}{2}$" (A)
> 1 piece – 3" x 36" x $\frac{1}{2}$" (B)
> 2 pieces – 16" x 36" x $\frac{1}{2}$" (C)
> 1 piece – 17" x 36" x $\frac{1}{2}$" (D)

An illustration showing how to cut the plywood appears on page 105.

To build the unit:

1. Nail the the two side pieces (16" x 36") to top and bottom pieces (12" x 16") as shown.

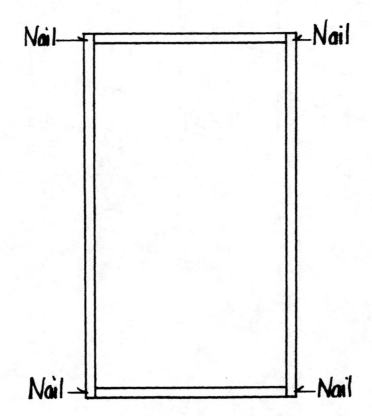

2. Measure down $1\frac{1}{2}$ " from the inside of the top panel and mark that location on a side panel. Repeat on the other side panel.

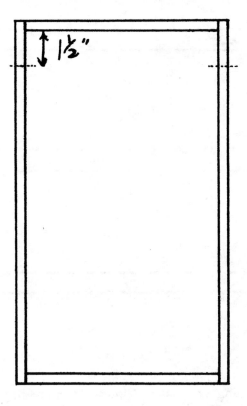

3. Place a 12" x 16" shelf in the unit so that the center of the shelf hits your marks. Nail it in.

4. Make another set of marks $1\frac{3}{4}$ "down from the first set of marks, and nail in another shelf.

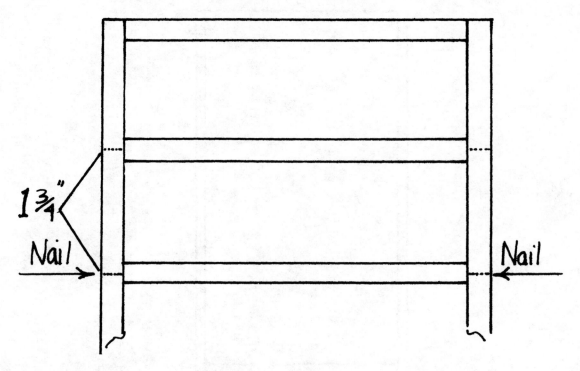

5. Continue making marks at $1\frac{3}{4}$ " intervals and nailing in shelves until you reach the bottom of the unit. There should be 20 slots with approximately $1\frac{1}{4}$ " between each slot.

6. Nail the 13" x 36" panel onto the back of the unit.

7. The 3" x 36" piece is nailed to the front of the unit. Label the slots on this piece with letters or numbers. This allows you to assign a slot to an individual student. See drawing on page 106.

Ideally, you would build enough units so that every student could have his or her own storage slot.

Slotted Storage Unit 1:
Cutting the Plywood

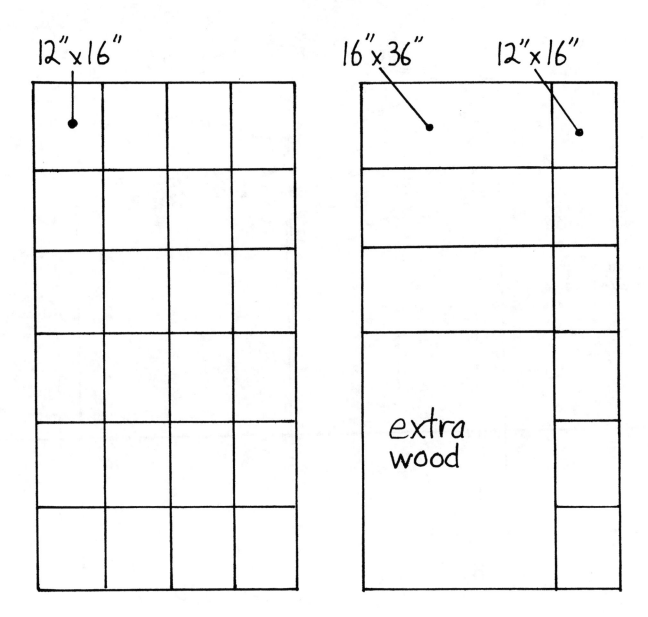

Slotted Storage Unit 2:
Assembling

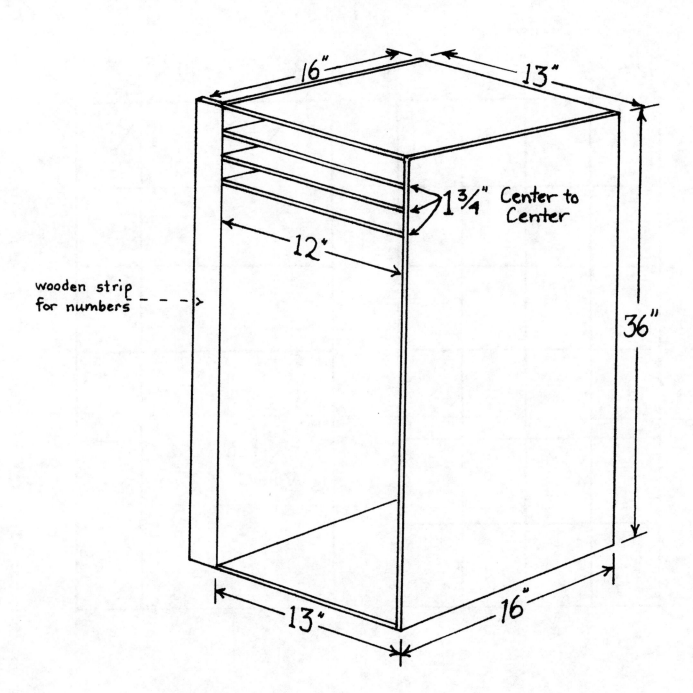

Slotted Storage Unit 3:
Finishing

Units for Finished Artwork
and Art to Be Returned

You can build units similar to the slotted storage unit for artwork that students are turning in to you or that you are returning to them. In each unit, you might put a slot for each class that you teach, or if you can build more units, for each tableful of students. Since the size of the units is up to you, I won't give detailed instructions for building them. You would use the same basic method described for the slotted storage unit.

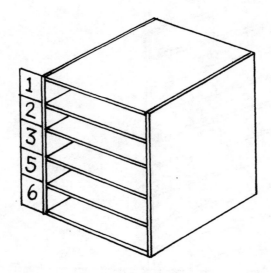

Finished artwork unit

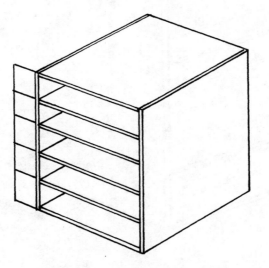

A unit for work to be returned to a class

Carving Block Holders

Here are the steps to construct a block holder for a right-handed person. Refer to the illustrations below for placement of the wood pieces.

1. Cut a 10" square piece of $\frac{1}{2}$" sanded plywood.

2. Cut a 10" piece of 1" x 2" wood. Any kind of wood will do, as long as it has these measurements.

3. Nail this piece to the square piece so that it is flush with one edge of the square.

4. Cut a piece of 1" x 2" wood 8" long and nail it to the square to form a 90° angle at the left end of the 1" x 2" x 10". (See diagram.)

5. Cut another piece of 1" x 2" wood 10" long. Nail it to the underside of the square. This bottom edge will hook over the front of the table to keep the block holder from moving while you are carving.

To construct a block holder for a left-handed person follow the same steps except that in step 4, you should nail the 1" x 2" x 8" piece to the *right* end. (See diagram.)

Here are the block holders side by side so that you can see the difference in construction:

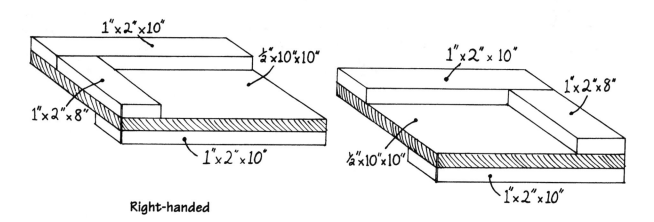

Right-handed

Left-handed

Here is how the block holder is used:

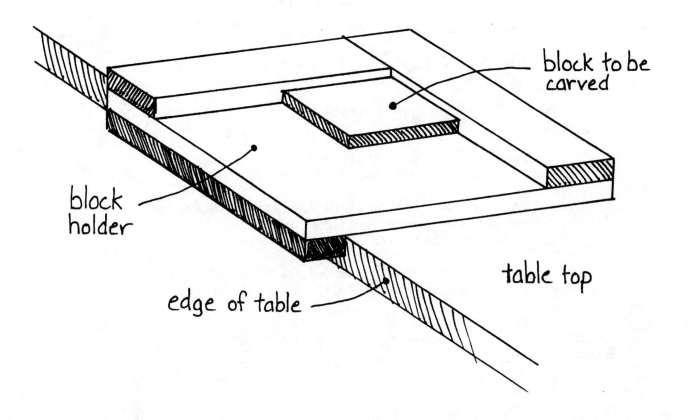

block to be carved

block holder

edge of table

table top

A Printing Block for
Two-Color Printing

To construct a printing block you will need the following:

> 1 piece of $\frac{3}{4}$ " plywood or particle board, 12" square
> 1 piece of wood 1" x 4" x 12"
> 1 piece of wood 1" x 4" x 8"
> 1 piece of wood 1" x 2" x 12"
> 1 piece of wood 1" x 2" x 9"

The steps are:

1. Nail the 1" x 4" x 12" piece of wood to the left side of the 12" x 12".

2. Nail the 1" x 4" x 8" piece of wood to the back edge of the 12" x 12" piece so that you form a 90° corner.

3. Draw a line 1" from the inside edge of the 1" x 4" x 12" piece. Nail one of the 1" x 2" x 12" along this line.

4. Draw a line 1" from the inside edge of the 1" x 4" x 12". Nail the 1" x 2" x 9" piece along this line to form a 90° angle with the 1" x 2" x 12".

The finished printing block will look like this:

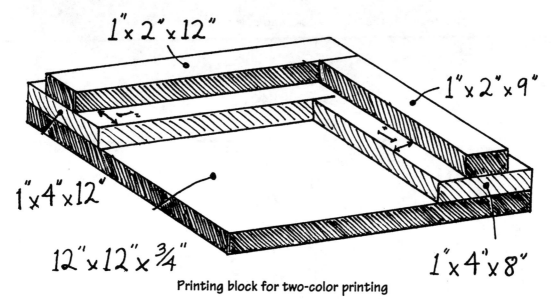

Printing block for two-color printing

Spray Box

To build a spray box (as discussed in Chapter 2, page 20; illustrated on page 21), you will need the following materials:

> 1 sheet of $\frac{3}{4}$ " particle board
> 1 pound of $1\frac{1}{2}$ " to 2" finishing nails
> 1 bathroom vent
> 4" stove pipe, enough to reach a window or other opening
>   to the outside of the building
> electrical cord to reach a nearby outlet

Before you begin to build, select a location for your spray box. It should be near a window where you can exhaust the fumes. Also, bear in mind that the installation will be more or less permanent, so choose a space that will not be needed later in the year.

To build the spray box (illustration on page 114):

1.   Cut the $\frac{3}{4}$ " particle board to these sizes:

     > 2 pieces 24" x $25\frac{1}{2}$ " (for front and back)
     > 4 pieces 24" x 24" (for top, bottom, and sides)

2.   Cut an opening in the front piece so you can put things into the box. Make it large enough for the largest object that you will be spraying.

3.   Nail together the front, back, and side panels as shown.

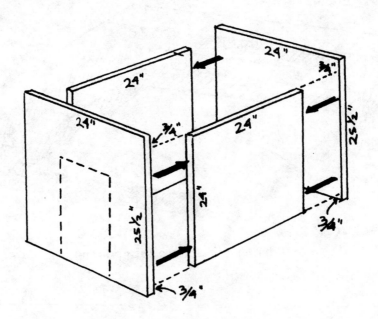

4. The bathroom vent should go in one of the upper corners in the back of the box. Cut a circle 5" in diameter in the corner you select. Also cut or drill a hole for the electrical cord. (See diagram.)

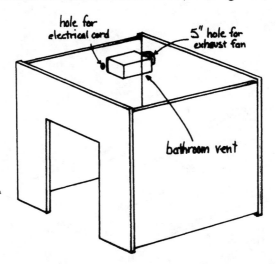

5. Make the electrical connection to the bathroom vent. Some vents come with wire in place, but if yours doesn't, and you don't know how to wire it, get help from the store salesperson, your shop teacher, or your custodian.

6. Mount the bathroom vent in the spray box and push the wire through the wire hole.

7. Nail on the top and bottom panels.

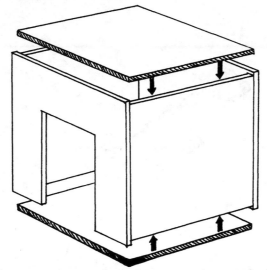

8. Connect the stove pipe to the exhaust opening on the bathroom vent and route the pipe to the window. If you have to run the pipe a long distance, you may need to support the pipe with wire or metal strapping.

Vented Spray Box

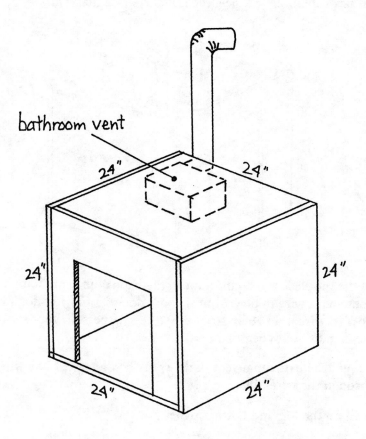

bathroom vent

24"   24"

24"   24"

24"   24"